THE HASSLE HANDBOOK

A Guide To Teenage Survival

THE HASSLE HANDBOOK

A Guide To Teenage Survival

by

John Frykman

REGENT
PRESS
Berkeley
California
1988

Published by
REGENT PRESS
2747 Regent Street
Berkeley, California 94705
(Individual copies may be ordered directly from Regent Press. Quantity discounts available to individuals and organizations as well as to bookstores. Write for information.)

ISBN: 0-916147-00-2

To Kristin, Lars, Erik, John, Mark, Sally, Jim, Linda, Sue, Betty, Norman, Lance, Michael, Lizzie, Miguel, Sarah, Melinda, Jonathan, Jesse, Rick, Barbara, Randy, Steven, Maria, Francy, Ellen, Laurette, Jerry, Duane, Scott, Francie, Lonzo, Leslie, Lois, Ken, Joe, Ricardo, Julie, Dianne, Bruce, Mary Ellen, Lisa, Peter, David — to mention but a few of the young people who have been directly involved in this book in one way or another. For their involvement, risk taking, skill, intelligence and love, I am grateful.

TABLE
OF
CONTENTS

Preface
GETTING
STARTED

This book is written for young people. It's aimed mainly at teenagers. Because of that, there should be a clear warning right here at the beginning!

CLEAR WARNING
Maybe you shouldn't read this book.
Why? It's been put together by an old
coot who is well into middle age. If that's
a problem for you, you'd better stop right now.

If you haven't trashed the book yet, I'll add that I've talked with a lot of young people about the things in this book, gotten their feedback, and paid attention to it. (This includes my own children: a daughter, and two sons.) I've spent lots of time being with young people, working with young people in a helping role, and being a young person myself (shaky days those were!). All parts of this book have been tested out with young people.

There were some, who came from big cities in the East, who said, "There are things I can't get with, like I've never seen lawns or lived in a suburb." There were some, who came from the country, who had very different reactions. So, don't expect that you will get with everything.

What is written here might open up a new way of dealing with those years when you are labelled "teenager," "adolescent," "young person," "child," or whatever other label someone might try to stick on you. For many people, it's a tough period.

The suggestions offered in this book have worked for some people. That doesn't mean that they will work for you. I believe, though, that once you put some of these suggestions into action, you will see changes. I think you'll find that by doing something concrete about problems, hassles, difficulties, hangups, you'll be handling more and more and more of your own problems without outside help.

I've tried to write things in such a way as not to take myself or what I'm writing about overly seriously. I hope you agree that humor often helps to make things more understandable, manageable, tolerable.

I'd like to say "thank you" to a number of people who have helped make this book possible; they have all given of their insight and knowledge in making this book more worthwhile. I'll describe what they do in life, but, most likely by the time this book comes out, many of them will be doing different things because they are such active and open people.

Cheryl Arnold has helped edit, given much of her soul and integrity to the whole process of putting the book together, and inspired me in so many ways I can't begin to count them. She is my lover and wife. Her experience includes community worker in inner-city racial ghettos, copywriter for a large urban "soul" radio station, a researcher on Youth Employment needs, church musician. She has written the chapter, "A Personal Account."

Jeffrey Whitmore has inspired, contributed to my sanity with his unending humor, and pushed me on with the work. He has been an editor, newspaper reporter, free-lance writer, novelist, and television writer. For this book he has written a few vignettes and contributed to the chapter on "Making Choices," and done the cartoons throughout the book.

Erika Krupp wrote the poem in the vignette section, "The Child," and is a student, poet and artist.

As for me, I am a licensed Marriage, Family and Child Counselor, Lutheran Minister, consultant, former director of an urban Drug Treatment Program, community counselor with a school district, homemaker (while living in England for three years), writer, and trainer.

Some of us who contributed to this book are members of a non-profit corporation, Cypress Institute of Monterey and San Francisco, California and Seattle Washington. It is organized to do research and training in the fields of human communication, education, therapy and problem solving, and to offer direct services to people in a problem solving way.

Presently I'm pastor of First United Lutheran Church in San Francisco, have a small private practice, and continue my consulting and training activities through Cypress Institute.

To Milton H. Erickson, M.D., Cheryl Arnold, Ron Cobley, John Weakland, Ingalill Osterberg, Meral Crane, Al Byrd, Richard Fisch, Jay Haley, Ric Masten, Rich Hawkins, Paul Watzlawick, Carl Segerhammar, Martin Heinecken, Toshiko Iba, Raila Kanisto, Tovio Rönka, Tappi Ahola, Betty Konstari, Tom Lehrer, David Wong, Herman van der Lippe, Eivind Rønn, Barry Bloom, Dorothy Beckwith, Leo Demarco, Jimmie Olson, Irv Shapiro, Paul Malone, John Butcher, Per August Kindberg, Jeff Whitmore, Rut Kindberg, Helmer, Ruth Maria, Bruce McSpadden, Miss Waite, Dale Lund, Saul David, Ted Williams, Doe Brousseau, Rod Duncan, Anne Frank, Bill Wenner, Fred Meyers, Evert Olson, Jim Daniels, Matthew Fox, J Jackson, Hong Qiao, Megan McKenna, Savio (Phil) Dindia, Claire Burch, Mark Weiman, Njal Petter, Anne Karine, Maude, Helmut, Charlotte, Niel, Jan, Linda, Nancy, Dwane, Jean, Mary, Howie, Judy, Ron, Billie, Barbara, Ruthie, Ed, Irene, Dan, Kim, Colleen, Linton — wherever you are, CHEERS! From all of you I've taken, to all of you I've given. In this giving and taking is the only meaningful life I have known. It's what happens between us that counts!

And that's what this book is really about — if it's just written words on a page, I'll be disappointed. The proof of what is here will be in what you do with my suggestions in relation to others, and how they respond to you.

Good luck!

John Frykman
Nov. 2 1983

Preface Postscript

This book is a revised version of an earlier edition published in Finland in 1979. It deals primarily with problem solving. A companion volume will soon follow dealing with decision making and practical guides to current issues like sex, drugs, consumer issues, health, etc.

PART I: THEORY – OF SORTS

Chapter 1
WHAT
ARE
HASSLES?

Hassles are the things that interfere with the way you want to live your life. A hassle can be anything that seems to block your ability to achieve certain kinds of goals.

Often when people are in trouble they tend to think that something is wrong with them. When I talk about hassles, I'm talking about something that has interfered with a person's ability to get along, not about something being wrong with the person!

Everybody has hassles, but *you* have more than your fair share. (I'm assuming *you* are a person somewhere between whenever and around 18.) One of the reasons that you have so many hassles is that you're constantly being given the message: "Grow up!"

The problem here is that if you just "grow up" as ordered, you haven't really "grown up." All you've done is prove that you're an obedient child who follows such confusing orders as: "Grow up!"

You may grow up long before you're accepted as a grownup, but you still have to deal with roadblocks. You don't have to "straighten out" so much as you have to find ways to get around the roadblocks.

When you're stuck with being a teen-ager — adolescent, juvenile, kid — you're undoubtedly stuck with being what you don't want to be, because what you want to be is a grown-up. Because everyone is telling you to "grow up" and at the same time denying you the right to exercise the act of growing up, you not only have hassles to overcome, you have far too many.

Not only do you have the hassles you create yourself — and all people create hassles for themselves — you also have the hassles caused by institutions that you didn't ask to be a part of such as your school, your church, the system of juvenile law, and so on.

You have a lot of hassles simply because of your age. There are things that are not hassles for adults, but are for you. Rightly or wrongly, the law says that you can't see certain movies — which adults can see — because you're not 18 or 21. And that's a hassle.

So what can you do? If, rather than having just the "right" attitude, you have the tools to create an option between various courses of action open to you, you can probably decrease the number of hassles to be contended with.

It's an age period that you've got to get through, and part of the purpose of this book is to show you ways to get past this period so you can relax or ways to relax so you can make it past.

I've known a lot of people who've been labeled "severely disturbed teen-ager." They've been told that the problem was within them — not with their parents, their school, their church, or the law — but that something was basically "wrong" with them. And then, surprisingly, when they get to be about 22 or so, everything starts going smoothly.

It's as though something magical has happened.

What actually happened isn't magic at all. It's just that they've begun to take care of themselves. Instead of having all sorts of solutions to their personal problems laid on them by other people, they've begun to solve their own problems themselves.

They've reached a time when they can solve their own problems. Most of the time the hassle wasn't the problem. It was what everyone else was doing to solve the problem that created the hassles.

Here's an example. You're walking down the street on a summer evening. You've just left a movie, haven't done anything wrong, and you're feeling good. At that moment a police car pulls up alongside you and the voice within it says:

"Why are you on the street, kid?"

"What do you mean?"

"It's after ten o'clock. Don't you know there's a curfew. Get in the car!"

So now there's a hassle.

You can say something like "leave me alone," or "Don't harass me," or come up with a lot of excuses — after all, that's what teenagers from the beginning have been trained to do by their parents and school.

Or you can respond to the policeman in a new way. You can say something like, "Gee, I'm sorry, I didn't realize it was after ten o'clock. What do you think I ought to do?"

Most of the time that will relieve the hassle. He might say, "Well, jump in and I'll give you a ride," or "Why don't you go right on home?" At any rate, because you've behaved in a new way, he's almost forced to behave in a new way, too.

People also get into hassles by thinking that the problems they are experiencing are the real problems. Most of the time, when a person has a hassle, it's not the hassle that's the hassle, but what the person is doing (or not doing) about the hassle.

An example: Got a teacher that is nasty, mean, a drag? Everything in class seems to be a downer? Well, what are you going to do about the hassle? You might bitch and moan to your friends about how bad things are. You might screw up in class just to break the monotony. You might cut class to avoid the whole mess. But most of the time these actions keep the whole vicious circle going, it gets worse and worse and worse. It's what *you* do about the hassle that keeps the hassle going, as well as what the teacher does.

I'll suggest some more direct ways of finding out *"how-to"* come up with plans to change things later in the book. But just for now what do you think would happen in the situation we've just discussed if you got to class a little early, went up to the teacher and said (whether it's true or not), "You know, I really like the fact that we've been having so many more class discussions lately."

My guess is that you would have a pretty good chance of having a class discussion that very day.

If you keep your cool, change what you are doing even a little bit, it's possible for the other person to change. In fact, we know from research that whenever people are in a relationship (interacting with each other), whether it is voluntary or involuntary, if one person changes what he is doing, the other person *has to change.* He has no choice.

For example, you know how people go through little ordinary greetings with each other. "Hi, how are you?" The usual response: "Fine, how are you?" or something similar. To see how true what I've said is, try a little experiment. The next time someone says "How are you?" answer, "Gee, I haven't thought about that. How do I look?" And pay attention to how the other person responds.

Here's another way to get a feeling for how important what you *do* is and how it can change things. Sometime when you get an uncomfortable feeling (a time when you are embarrassed, afraid, uptight, angry, you know the times that make you uncomfortable) instead of doing what you would *usually* do, stop. Catch yourself. Count to ten. And then consciously decide to do something *different* from what you *usually* do.

Watch what happens. Pay attention to what happens to you and to other people that you are with.

Example: If when you get angry at someone you usually launch into fighting, swearing, or whatever, stop, count to ten, and then ask the person with whom you are angry to explain their position. You might say something like, "I'm not so sure I can see your point of view, but I'd like to try. Would you run it by me again?" In the words of the song, "Watch what happens." I think you'll be surprised.

One of the things that all of this means is that when it comes to dealing with people-related hassles, common sense almost always makes things worse. To make things better, try a little uncommon sense.

Your boy/girl friend thinks you've been cheating. Common sense response: All sorts of excuses and explanations to prove he/she is wrong and that you haven't really been cheating. Usual result: More suspicion that needs more answers that cause more suspicion that results in fights, arguments, whatever.

Uncommon sense in that situation might tell you to say, "I guess there's no real way I can prove I've been faithful, even though I have. I hope you're not too upset and that you'll find out that your suspicions are really unnecessary. What made you feel that way, anyway?"

And then carefully stay clear of making any excuses explaining your side of the issue. Be a good listener.

Another illustration: You arrive home late. Parents are waiting to scold. You walk in the door: "Why are you late again?"

Common sense response: A whole set of excuses and explanations which many times are very far from the truth because you know that your parents cannot take the straight facts, and there is an inevitable escalation that ends in whatever way it usually ends in your house.

Uncommon sense knows that almost no explanation that you can have in this situation is going to be acceptable. Even if it's legitimate, because of how long this kind of thing has been going on in your house, there is going to be some anguish. What needs to be changed is the game. Remember, if *you* change, *they* are going to have to change; they have no choice. Maybe not the first time you try, but if you stay with it and stay cool, they'll change. What you do makes a difference.

An example of a different response in this situation: Beat them to the punch. before they ask "*Why?*" before they say a word, you say, "I know, I'm late and I'm sorry. I don't have any excuses. How can I make up for it?" And then be quiet, just listen, no excuses, stay cool, keep your head, just get to bed as fast as you can without walking out on them.

Remember, by *doing* acts like these, you will be changing your parents' behavior in a way that starts to make things better for you. They will start to get the message (without you ever saying a thing) that you really are mature, that you are able to take care of yourself. And they will start to relax a little more.

Another way to avoid the coming home late hassle is always to say that you are going to stay out a half-hour later than you really wish or intend to. Then even if you come home fifteen minutes late by your timetable, you will be fifteen minutes early by the one set up with your folks, and they will be pleased.

"My word," they might say, "he/she can't think it's so awfully bad around here; he/she's home fifteen minutes before time." Score one for you!

I've said that what you *do* about a hassle is what makes a difference in *getting past* the hassle. I also feel that the way you *look* at a hassle has a lot to do with whether you *can do* anything different about it.

For example: If you *look* at your parents (or teacher or whomever) as being hopeless, they probably will end up being hopeless. If you *look* at your situation in school as being hopeless, it will probably live up to your expectations. If you *look* at yourself as being sick in the head, you will more than likely end up acting that way.

On the other hand, if you take the position: *"Maybe* it is hopeless, but I'm going to try to do things a little differently and see what happens," you'll find that you can get past with greater ease more and more of the daily hassles that come your way.

The key word here is *maybe.* By saying "maybe" you keep the situation open. You don't get locked into that feeling of inevitable failure, which usually leads to more frustration and more hassles.

You'll find suggestions for "doing things differently" in this book, and you'll probably be able to expand them by using your ingenuity to help solve your own personal hassles.

Some situations *are* hopeless. (We'll talk about some of these in a later chapter and try to suggest ways to survive them.) But most situations — hassles — are not hopeless. They only get put in the hopeless bag because of how we *look* at them and what we *do* about them.

Chapter 2
GOING THROUGH CHANGES
(Or learning to deal with the Hollywood-Hippy Dream)

MR. MERKIN, MASTER
RÔLE - PLAYER.

A lot of people have the idea that the way life should be is "smooth and happy and peaceful and calm and without problems." And that if their lives are not like that, somehow there is something wrong. It's the way of looking at things that I like to call the Hollywood-Hippy-Dream — a dream of a utopian world with no trouble.

Of course, if you buy into that kind of a view of things, and your life is *not* trouble-free and smooth, you must do something drastic about it. And people try a lot of funny things.

They might run away — not just kids, but adults, too! They might try to blot out the trouble with booze or drugs. They might stay in a down place wallowing in their hopelessness and, in that way, not face what's happening. They might pretend that they are in utopia by participating in some far-out religious cult. They might make all their actions revolve around one activity to give them the feeling that "it's all cool," like a car, motorcycle, surfing, the street scene, sports, music, or like endeavors.

There are many ways a person tries to say to himself, "Hey, it's all OK. I've got it all nailed down."

Now that might be possible for you — maybe it is for a few people. But I have a different view of things. To me, "making it" is not so much being without problems as it is the ability a person has to deal with his/her own fair share of hassles. To me, life is to a large extent made up of dealing with the difficulties that come our way. Sure, we have some level places where it all seems pretty cool and groovy, but we're in pretty bad shape if we're thrown for a loop any

9

time an ordinary daily hassle comes our way.

We need to learn how to handle hassles, and that's what this little book is all about. Who wants to go into a six-month depression just because they've lost their boy/girl friend? And yet, that's what happens to many people.

What I'm trying to say is that the quality of one's life is not measured by just how free that life is of hassles; an even more important measure is how well one deals with his fair share of hassles, problems, hang-ups, or whatever you want to call them.

One of the things that can help give you a way to deal with the ordinary hassles that come up is to learn that most of the time hassles come up when people are *going through changes,* the time some might call, "Game Time." If you can be aware of this, you really don't have to do much about the hassle except to find a way to get on the other side of the changes.

Now, what in the world is meant by going through changes? There are events that happen as we live our lives that have a built-in potential for trouble. A lot of these changes are welcome. This often makes it more difficult for us to deal with hassles that go with them.

One event which we might call "going through changes" is when a man and woman focus their attention on each other and become a couple. They both want it. They are happy about it. And yet, so many times there's trouble.

"John, Doris said she saw you walking down the street with Alice the other day. What's the story?"

And there you have a hassle. All kinds of struggles, hurts, competitions can develop until the couple either settles down and relaxes as a couple, or splits up. In either case, they have "gone through changes."

I think that you can already see how much easier it would be if you said to each other, "Hey, it's great to be together, but we'll probably have some bumps to get over before being with each other is really going to seem right." This is a little strategy that can help a person go through changes a bit easier.

There are many more of these transitions — times when people go through changes that are just as difficult to deal with. You can have hassles because your mother and father are having trouble, because they're going through changes in their relationship. Often you can get caught in the middle and be blamed for lots of things. You might begin to act in crazy ways because you notice that they stop fighting when you're in trouble, and they focus on helping you.

If your parents get divorced, that's one of these changes. It affects you, too. What happens when Dad wants you to come and spend the weekend with him when it's time for the big dance or the homecoming game? Or what happens when Mom or Dad decides to remarry—and you don't know what to do? You're being forced to face up to going through changes that you haven't asked for.

What if a new child comes into the house? Again the balance of the family is upset, even if the child is desired by everyone. The family is upset, even if the child is desired by everyone. The family is in the position of going through changes again before it settles down.

When you move to a new community and have to get used to new schools and friends, it's another of those times you go through changes. Sometimes it's difficult, sometimes not so difficult, but always there's the potential for hassles.

Learning how to deal with a death in the family or the death of a friend, involves going through changes.

When you go away to boarding school or off to college or into military service, you go through changes — you learn to deal with life in a new way. And it's never the same as it used to be. Each transition adds something to what we are, and we either become more capable of dealing with hassles or less capable. It's very, very difficult to stay the same in the face of change.

Having a baby (wanted or not) or getting a woman pregnant, means going through changes — and these changes can often affect what goes on in your life for a good deal of time.

There are many changes that all of us have to go through. It can really help if, when things are starting to go bad, a person can step back and say, "Hey, what's happening here? Is there some change I or my family is going through that I need to get past?" Because in many instances you don't need to solve hassles, you just have to get past them. Once past, or once through the changes, things tend to settle down to be all right until you reach another set of changes.

To look at it graphically:

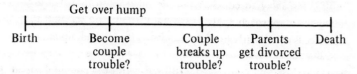

The task, very simple, is getting over the hump to where things settle down again. When you anticipate possible trouble that can come with an expected change, you can often minimize that trouble and cut down the amount of time that is necessary to get over the hump into the settled place.

One of the proofs of this whole idea is that the last transition that people have to deal with is death, and surprisingly to some people, though not to me, most people deal with this transition with very little difficulty. To me it means that everyone gears up for this transition, no one expects it to be easy, everyone rallys around to help the grieving people, and so the hassles involved in getting over the hump are relatively easy for the family to cope with.

Again, as I have mentioned many times before, people don't have hassles alone. *Hassles always happen in the context of interpersonal relationships.*

Coming up with things to do about hassles — things to help get you over the hump of a particular change that you are going through — always involves *doing* something which involves others.

There is one final example of going through changes that is very important to deal with. And almost every family that has ever lived on this earth has had some difficulty in dealing with this change. It is the transition that takes place when a child — especially the first child begins to move out of the house and becomes independent.

This is a real threat to the organism that is the family. And the organism usually responds in a way *intended* to keep itself together, but one that often leads to a rupturing of the organism that is very difficult to repair.

This change can start when a child is very young — whenever he/she wants to make decisions for him/herself, sometimes as early as

10 or 11 years of age. More commonly, the effect of this transition occurs at the beginning of high school, near graduation from high school, going away to college or into military service, or when a person begins to approach that magical age of 18, legal adulthood. This last change is particularly hard to deal with in many family situations.

Some of the ways that families reach out, grab on, and try to keep the threatening member from partially separating from the organism are very subtle.

Mom might buy you an aluminum mailing case in which to send your laundry back and forth from college. That's her way of saying that you're still part of the household, only now your bedroom is in the college dorm.

Fathers, especially, have a way of coming down with all sorts of rules and regulations for daughters who are approaching the age of 18. And it's all under the guise of protecting them or helping them to grow up.

In many cases he remembers how he acted with girls when he was in high school and he doesn't want boys acting that way with you. (A little thing you might try here: Say to him, person-to-person, "Dad, I'm having a little difficulty knowing how to act with boys. Would you be willing to level with me about how you acted with girls in high school?")

I could give a lot more examples of specific things that families do to deal with this "set of changes," but I don't think it's necessary. Just be aware. If things are particularly uptight around your house, step back, look at what's going on, see if maybe the hassles that you are experiencing are tied to this very basic change, the change caused by your becoming independent, your beginning the move out of the family house. The same thing, of course, can occur when one of your brothers or sisters is in that spot.

If that's what's happening, the task is not to cure a sick family, to help the family communicate better, or to tell the parents to feel better about their kids growing up. You simply have to get over the hump, to go through this very difficult transition, and then settle down and relax.

And what are some of the types of things that you can do to help your family get through this set of changes when you are striving for independence? Try these:

1. *"Keeping it out on the table."* When you're having meals together, or just having talks with your parents, don't talk about the trouble your family has in dealing with this. That would make them uptight. Instead, talk about how much trouble so-and-so's family is having letting their son/daughter grow up, and tell them how glad you are that it is possible to talk about those things in "our family."

2. *"Maybe you're right."* Lots of times parents in this situation have a tendency to come down really hard on kids with all kinds of advice and instructions. Statements that begin with "you should," "you'd better," "you ought," "I think that," "let's," "we feel that," and so on make the back of your neck start to get squirmy, and you know a lug is about to be laid on you. If you can keep your cool and respond with something like, "Maybe you're right, Dad, could you try to explain that to me again so I can try to understand?" You'd be surprised at how quickly things start to change. You begin to be in control, not your folks.

Please notice that you are not copping out, you are not saying "you are right," only *"Maybe* you are right." When you argue with a parent who is coming on in that way, the only thing the parent can do to keep his/her dignity is to win the argument with you. The "maybe you're right" tactic gives them a little room to change or modify their position to one closer to yours.

3. *"I'm not so sure."* This is a modification of "maybe you're right." If it's really coming heavy, sometimes getting a little time can make all the difference. "I'm not so sure about that, Dad. Would you be willing to give me a little time to think about it?"

This can often be very disarming. It can also demonstrate your maturity.

4. *"I'm really confused."* When in the heat of this set of changes you can't think of anything to do, "I'm really confused," can relieve a lot of pressure. The important thing is to stay away from giving your reasons for things to your parents, because in this uptight set of changes, no matter how valid your reasons, they are not usually acceptable.

5. *"Doing the unasked for."* Another strategy that gets parents over this hump is for you to do things that show you are really responsible. Don't tell them that you are doing the things, but make sure that they know you are. These don't have to be big deal things, either. They can be things like sending birthday cards to grandparents; have a meal with candlelight and the works ready when the folks get home; phoning them to tell them you think you might be getting home a little early (see above); asking their advice about something you're going to do (like buying a car or choosing a college). You don't have to take the advice, just ask for it.

Another type of thing you could do is to take them out for dinner to a nice restaurant — paying the bill yourself. Or you could get permission to use the family car and then come back a short while later and say that you've decided to take the bus to save wear and tear on the car.

In other words, use your imagination to do things that demonstrate — without your saying anything about it — that you are, in fact, able to take care of yourself.

I haven't covered the whole waterfront with respect to the very important area of changes we go through. But I've tried to open you up to the idea that a lot of times all that's necessary to get past a hassle is to develop some small task, something to do, something to say, that will help those involved get over the hump. Once over it, things can settle down and flow.

Good luck as you try some strategies yourself.

Chapter 3
SOLVING PROBLEMS AND MAKING DECISIONS

Solving Problems

For a long time I've been trying to come up with ways young people can deal with problems without needing help from others. I'm not sure I've found ultimate answers, but I know that the process I'll describe here is one that has worked in many situations. Even though what I suggest might seem a little crazy at times, and common sense might say, "That won't work," or you might say, "I've already tried that," I think that if you pick up on the spirit of these suggestions and experiment with them in small ways you'll start having some success and maybe some surprises.

Here's something that surprised me when I began noticing it: With most people, their main problem is not their main problem. Instead, their "solutions" are the main problem. In fact, all the things people do to try to solve a problem can change it from an ordinary hassle into a serious problem. What I will outline here is a step-by-step way to change what you're doing about a problem, thus changing the problem itself, and, hopefully, get things moving toward real change.

There is a lot of value in small changes. If you pay attention to what's happening with people, you'll see that if one person changes some usual way of acting, even in a small way about a small thing, all the other people involved will change, too. We all get into patterns with each other, and if one person does something out of the ordinary, there's no way the rest can fail to respond. We get a little off-balance, maybe shift gears, and that's when something new can happen. For example, two kids grow up close together, compete and quarrel a lot over possessions; then, one day, the older one who's gotten to be about 14, stops in mid-quarrel and says, "I don't feel like fighting. You can have it." There's no way the other can keep on acting the same way.

A change is not necessarily an improvement. But if you change what you're doing about a problem, the other people involved will change their response toward you. You will then have new information, allowing you to plan more specifically what you could do next to resolve that problem.

Step One

Sometimes it takes a little thought to know what directions to take. Everybody has problems; there is no one without problems. A common mistake that people make is to try to work on all their problems at once, which almost never works. You have a better chance of success if you first choose one problem to focus on, and really clarify it. As far as I'm concerned, it's best to choose what you consider to be your toughest problem, not a minor one. It's good to have a little notebook, too. Write down your thinking as you're going through these steps. It will really help to make the process a lot more efficient. What would be most important to deal with, what would make the most difference in your life — if you could change it even slightly? In focusing on one problem, it's very important to clarify it, to state what is happening with it in concrete terms. Then you'll be able to know if you're making any progress with that problem.

Let me give you an example. A person may identify his problem as "being depressed." That's very difficult to deal with because a person can easily label almost any bad feeling as depression. Without realizing, a person can get into "being depressed" 95 percent of the time because any bad feeling is labeled as a problem, and that problem is called "depression."

I'd suggest that if you call your problem "depression," go a step further and ask yourself, "What happens to me when I get depressed? Does anything seem to trigger it? What are people saying to me when

I get depressed? By getting more specific, you can set a more specific goal for solving your problem. You might say, "I always cry when I get depressed." It's easier to know if you've solved that problem — it's easier to know if you're crying or not — than if you're depressed or not. Or you might say, "Well, when I get depressed I don't want to see anybody, so I stay by myself. I isolate myself." Again, you have clarified the problem. You can start getting a handle on it just by paying attention to being or not being with people. You can clarify a problem by describing it as something you do, rather than by labeling it "depression."

Step Two

Go further with these "what is happening" questions. "Who is involved with me when I'm experiencing this problem? Are my parents involved, boyfriend or girl friend, brother, sister, teacher, boss — who is involved? What are they doing? What am I doing? How do they react? What do I do then?" When you run down the normal sequence of events of your problem, do you see clues — some little change you could work on that might lead to more significant change?

Step Three

Think about *now*. Has anything forced you do deal with the problem *now?* Is it important to deal with it *now?* Has someone given you an ultimatum: "Shape up or else!" (or else you'll go to a hospital, a psychiatrist, juvenile hall, whatever). Often the answer to these "now" questions can help you see a way to deal with a problem. Here's an example: If your parents are pushing you to solve a problem, you need to get them off your back — or you won't be able to deal with it. One thing you might say to them is something like, "Well, Mom and Dad, I agree with you that I need to deal with it, so I'm going to see the school counselor on Monday." You have given them a way to relax a little and take some heat off you, because they see you taking action. Seeing a school counselor might not solve anything, but it might give you some time and space to come up with another plan on your own.

Step Four

Most important: What "solutions" have you already tried? Most of us, when we have a problem, try a number of solutions that fail and make the problem seem worse. Take time to list all the things you have been doing about a problem. Take pains also to list what other people have been doing about it. To continue with the "depressed" illustration, have you been trying to fight it off? (Sometimes trying to fight off an emotion brings it on stronger.) Have you tried to be with friends when you're depressed? Have you talked with a school counselor? With friends? With your parents? What have your friends and relatives and parents done? Has anyone talked to you about it? Do people treat you cautiously, as if you're a little "sick"? Have your friends been commiserating with you? Have they tried to cheer you up? (Trying to cheer up someone can often make things worse.) List everything you can remember that you and others have done to solve your problem. Write specifically and clearly. At the least, you will learn which solutions have not worked, so can plan a *new* strategy for yourself.

Step Five

Now you are ready to take action, to come up with a plan, something that *you're* going to *do* about the problem. This "something that you're going to do" means a plan of action, specific actions that you will do for a limited period of time. Make a decision how long you'll give the plan. A week? A few days? Longer?

The limited time is important because it will help you focus on your plan. If your plan is working, you can know that clearly. If it is not working, you will not have experienced a giant defeat. You can simply recycle the plan, revise, change, whatever, for another limited time period. Usually, I would suggest that a plan be for no longer than a week, sometimes less, if you're really hurting and need some progress quickly. The point is to set up your plan with the awareness that *it* might fail, but *you* will not have failed. At the outset, the smaller the plan, the better. The less you upset your life, the better.

In the example of depression, a possible plan (which is not to say it would be right for everyone) is to say, "Well, maybe it isn't all that bad to be depressed. Maybe my body and my mind are trying to tell me something when I get depressed. Instead of fighting depression, maybe I should go with it for a while. Whenever I feel a depression coming on, I'll allow myself to be depressed for five minutes. During that time, I'll concentrate and listen to what's going on with my head. At the end of five minutes, I'll shrug my shoulders, shake my head, stand up, leave the room, and go do something that is usually a happy trip for me. I'll try this plan faithfully for one week, and then I'll evaluate how it's worked." In this kind of plan, it would be important to give your full energy to the five minutes of depression, and then to give your full energy to physically moving out and on to a different activity. For example, go for a walk, play tennis, listen to music, ride your bike, drive your car, talk to a friend — just be sure it's an active change of pace.

This simple problem-solving design which I've described is based on a belief that "problem" does not mean "something wrong inside one's head." Usually, a person with a problem has got stuck in some situation, often with other people and simply getting unstuck will start things moving toward solving the problem. You need not aim for a total solution. Rather, aim for some movement, some change. In this way you'll open up new possibilities, and you'll be coping. You will be unstuck.

Further Suggestions

1. When you're going through the five steps above, keep your eyes and ears alert to anything that seems to come up again and again — maybe a word, a phrase, a complaint, a wish or frustration, a physical gesture, expression or mannerism. Anything that is a powerful pattern also carries power for change. For example, every time you come home late, your mother says, "Why are you home late?" (This sets you up to respond in a certain way, because it's an accusation, not really an authentic question.) Every time your mother says, "Why are you home late?" you come up with an excuse which you have already rehearsed, and which may be more related to what you think she will accept than to what is true. But the excuses never seem to work. Your mother gives you the same lecture every time — and

you give the same response. One way you might start some change in this powerful pattern is to say, "Gee, Mom, I'm really sorry. I know how you worry. What do you think I should do to make this less of a problem for you?"

2. Another place to look for a problem-solving clue is where you see a power struggle going on. Often arguments get nowhere because each person is stubbornly stuck on proving he or she is right. No one can win. A deadlocked power struggle like this is a good place to try the "maybe you're right" principle. Here's how it works: Someone is coming on strong, sucking you into an argument he/she intends to win. Resist the temptation to express your point of view. instead, say, "Well, maybe you're right, but could you run over that again...?" He probably will. Resist disagreement once more, replying: "Well, yeah, but that part is confusing to me. Could you explain it in a little different way?" By this time, you've significantly defused what could have been an explosive argument. You probably have reassured the person that you respect his point of view. You might even have relaxed him enough that he will be able to come around a little bit toward your point of view, without seeing it as a loss of face.

Saying "maybe you're right" is not saying "you are right." It's not copping out, or giving up your own point of view. But it is a way to recognize the other person's point of view, so that you have a chance to come across with yours. The other side of the coin is "maybe you're wrong."

3. If your problem involves somebody else whom you would like to influence in changing certain ways, ask yourself: "Is there any way I could get so-and-so to do the opposite of what she's doing now, while it seems like she's doing the same thing she's always done?" (You're right — it's quite a trick.) An example: Your father continually criticizes you. You alternately defend yourself, mope, and fight with him. Next time, ask for the criticism: "Dad, I know I screwed up again. I know it upsets you. But I guess part of the problem is I just don't understand what you expect. Maybe if you told me just exactly what it is I do wrong, just exactly what you want me to do . . . " In other words, ask him to do what he's been doing all along. But, of course, you've never asked for it before, so you might be

surprised at how you have begun a change in interaction.

4. If your problem is something that *happens,* and that happens often, look closely at the events that usually come before and after. For example, if your problem is getting into continual hassles, fights, with your girlfriend, think about the last few you've had and what were the events that immediately preceded and followed the fights. You might also think about the times when you're able to deal with difficulties without getting into fights. Maybe you'll realize that there's some pattern, or maybe one little thing that always seems to happen before you get into fighting. In that case, next time you might be able to see the storm signals before the storm is upon you. Instead of just getting sucked in, you might be able to say something like, "Hey, it looks like we're heading for a fight again. If we're going to do it, let's do it now — let's get into it right now and get it over with." This will change the game. You might still fight, but it will be different — you might pick up some new clues on how to solve the problem. You might even decide you don't need to fight.

These are just a few ideas. You'll find many other examples scattered throughout this book. The key thing is to find some way to change what you're doing about the problem you want to work on. This is a fact of human relationships: If you change what you are doing, the people that you are involved with have to change in some way, too.

Making Decisions

This five-step process of solving problems can also be used to prevent problems from developing — by giving you a handle on dealing with important things, taking charge of your life, instead of just letting it happen to you.

Take the example of making an important decision. One value of planning is to allow yourself some time. If you feel you're in the middle of a crisis, ask yourself, "Could I possibly wait until tomorrow to decide about this?" Usually you can; and seldom are good decisions made in the middle of a crisis. Don't make a decision in the heat of battle unless you have no choice. The next morning, things will probably be less uptight, and your head will be freer to think and deal with that situation.

When you have given yourself a little time to work on making a decision, sit down with paper and pencil and ask yourself what you need to know first. Write down what you already know; what you need to find out; pros and cons; or, if you are making a choice between two alternatives, the pros and cons of each. This can be used in making just about any decision whether it's continuing a romance, choosing courses to take, maintaining an unpleasant job, relating to parents or teachers, whatever. After you've made your list, do your homework: take time to find out what else you need to know. Also, set yourself a day and time when you should get it all together and decide.

When the time comes to make the decision, you probably will find your head a lot clearer than before, and your confidence increased, even if it's a tough issue. Do it — but don't make it a forever thing. Choose a time period (a week, a month, six months, whatever) that seems right for you, a time in which you can stick to your decision, and then evaluate it afterward. Many people cause themselves a lot of unnecessary pain by imagining that they're stuck with a decision they've made. If you can set up ahead of time a reasonable way to change your mind, it might be easier to make decisions in the first place.

In a nutshell, what I've been saying about solving problems is this: It's what you *do* that gets you in and out of trouble, not what you feel or think, or wonder about; and there's no way the people involved with you can stay the same if you change what you're doing about a problem.

I hope you'll try some of these suggestions to start getting a sense of what they can accomplish. Remember, focus on *what* is happening, not why it's happening. Focus on finding a small way in which you can begin to get unstuck from what has become a hang-up. You'll be finding ways to handle your problems, rather than letting them handle you.

There are no "solutions," only beginning steps (actions) toward solutions.

Chapter 4
NOTES
ON
PERSONAL
SURVIVAL

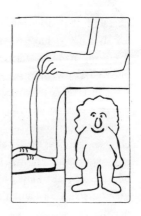

Much of what is written in this book falls into neat categories . . . raising children, parent hassles, friendship hang-ups, medical problems.

But there are some things that can help a person deal with hassles that don't fit into such neat categories. They are what this chapter is all about.

What do you do when you're up against impossible situations? What do you do if you're alone in a big city in danger of being assaulted? What do you do if you don't have a place to stay and don't have food? These are notes for personal survival when you get into situations that are unfamiliar, where you have no previous coping experience.

First, let's discuss hopeless situations. For the most part, hopeless situations all fall into the same kind of bag. They are the kind of situations that are usually described as EITHER/OR — *either* my parents get off my back and leave me alone *or* I'm going to run away from home. *Either* I learn how to get along with girls and friends *or* I'm going to commit suicide. *Either* (you know what to put here) *or* (and here). You know what it is for you. It comes up time and time again.

Many times these situations *seem* totally hopeless. You're trying to get permission from your parents to do something that you know is cool and OK, but they won't even talk about it. They just heavy-handedly say, "No!" Or a teacher makes a demand, "Make up all that work *or* you flunk." Or your girlfriend/boyfriend puts it, "*Either* you move out from your folks and into a room with me, *or* it's all

24

over between us.''

Now maybe *some* of these situations *will* turn out to be impossible. Hopeless! But there *are* some tactics that can be employed as delaying actions that sometimes open up these either/or situations.

Tactic Number One

Get some space, get out of the uptight, up-against it place for a short time and see what happens. An example of this with heavy-handed parents is that instead of continuously trying to reason with them to see it your way, back off. Don't do anything for three days. If the parent continues to give you unwanted advice, don't argue; draw the parent out instead. "I'm not so sure I understand, tell it to me again." Be sure not to use sarcasm though; that almost always backfires.

Another variation of Tactic One: Just be very quiet. Don't speak unless spoken to, play as though you are very involved in heavy thinking or reading while you are around the house. Play a different kind of music (maybe classical) on the radio or phonograph than you usually do. I think you will be amazed how often this will bring about some small changes in the way people respond to you, whether they be parents, teachers, or friends. It changes the "normal" balance.

Tactic Number Two

Find someone reliable whom you can talk to who is not of your own age. It should be someone that is at least five years older or younger than you. Someone you know is not going to tell anyone else what you tell them.

The difference in age is very important because a lot of times people who are the same age and talk to each other are caught in the same binds. They only increase the feelings of hopelessness in each other.

I *don't* mean for you to take advice from this person. Taking advice from friends can often be disastrous, mostly because they suggest things that may have worked for them. Every person is a unique individual, and what works for one person doesn't always, or even usually, work for another. You have a different father, mother, set of teachers and friends, than the person you're talking to.

So just use the person as a sounding board. It's a good way of clarifying your own mind, but again, don't look for advice. (I've found that sometimes the most reliable person for a lot of the teenagers I know is a person late in age, past 60, who is not part of their family, someone you've learned is "approachable" and trustworthy.)

Tactic Number Three

Permission to say "no." A hard-nosed teacher is making unreasonable demands. You want to find a way through to the teacher and you say to him/her: "I'd like to ask you something, but I know even before I do that what I'm going to ask is one of those things that you don't usually go for. I can respect that. So before I even ask, I want you to know it is OK with me if you say no. Would you be willing to give me two extra days to get this assignment in?"

What this does, of course, is to change the usual game. By your action, the teacher might be able to look at you in a new way. If he's one who needs to be in control, he has to say "yes" to stay in control. Another possibility is that it might throw him off balance enough so that he'll come up with a totally new option for getting out of the either/or situation. This kind of strategy is also effective with parents. Sometimes it will not work the first time, but if you continue to try, maybe on another issue a few days later, usually there will be a change, even if it is only a willingness for some other kind of compromise, and that's a step ahead.

Tactic Number Four

Going with it. Many times when people feel that they are in impossible situations, the situations are heightened because the people become constantly obsessed with them. They continuously talk about them; wallow in them; and make the impossible situations seem (and often become) much more serious than they started out to be.

Now what I'm about to suggest is going to sound absolutely crazy, and because it does sound that way it might be pretty hard for you to try! Because I know there are some young people willing to try what seems a little far out, I'll put this on the table in two variations.

First variation. Instead of letting all the things that concern you about your own desperate situation haunt you all day, consolidate the haunting into specific time spans. It's natural and normal to have bad feelings, but not to have them all the time. So allow yourself the dignity of recognizing your bad feelings and set aside some time — at least four times a day — to give them recognition.

Pick a place where you can be alone for at least 5 minutes or as long as 15 minutes. Then really "go with it." Get into agnozing as deeply as you can about your impossible situation. You might do it once in the morning when you wake up; again around noon; once more around supper-time; and again sometime during the evening.

After the 5-, 10-, or 15-minute period is up (you might decide on 7½ minutes — it's up to you), shrug your shoulders, shake it off, and set the agnozing on the shelf until the next time it's due. Then go do something you like to do. I know it sounds a little crazy, but it could be well worth your trying. (Better not let anyone know, though, for they might thing you're ready for the booby hatch!)

Second variation. Instead of agonizing four times a day, agonize about it (your hopeless, impossible situation) for just two minutes every time it pops into your mind or consciousness. At the end of the two minutes, shake it off and do something you like to do, or talk to someone you like to talk to.

These suggestions might be very difficult for many of you to get with, but if you do try them, I think you might be very surprised by what happens.

Another valuable aspect of personal survival is knowing what to do when you're in a strange place. Sometimes you might take off for a weekend in the big city, and things can get a little out of control. You might lose your money or have it ripped off. A friend who was with you might turn around and go home, leaving you alone. All kinds of things can happen that can turn what was to be a fun trip into a nightmare.

The ideas which follow are some things that people who have had experience living in cities and other strange places (and home can be a strange place, too) have learned. They learned them because they had to in order to survive. You can learn so that if you are caught in an unfortunate circumstance you can keep it and get it TOGETHER. These are going to be random snapshots of things you might run up against. There's no particular order, just a jumble of things to think about, to learn.

You're walking alone in a deserted part of town when two dudes come toward you on the sidewalk. They part, very politely, to let you walk between them — don't do it! I did once and wound up with some bruises and minus my wallet. Go out around them on the street side, never up close to the building.

You're in a restaurant that isn't exactly the Ritz Plaza, but you're in there because it's the cheapest place you can find and you don't have much money. As you sit there looking at the back wall, suddenly someone puts his arm around your neck and drags you out of the restaurant. It might be someone trying to rip you off. It might be the police who've found you from your parents' lost person report. Moral: It's safer to sit facing the entrance door to the restaurant; at least you can see what's coming up.

There are other good reasons for this, too. The French know about this — all their sidewalk restaurants have the chairs facing out to the sidewalk so you can see who's passing by. If you sit facing the door — the outside — you have a better chance to pick up on the vibes in the place, good or bad. You can watch your coat or hat or pack better as well — just good sense all around. If you have a friend with you and your back's to the door, clue her in to it, and sit back and relax and have fun.

You've got no money, no place to stay, it's getting late in the day, you don't know anyone to call in the city, and you don't much like the idea of sleeping out-of-doors. Where can you go?

My experience indicates one of the safest maneuvers is to go to a clergyperson. But it isn't enough just to go to one blind. Do a little homework before you leave home. Get the name of the pastor, maybe your own, of one of the major denomination churches in your community before you leave home. Better yet, get to know a pastor, rabbi or priest. Write his/her name and the name of the church and denomination on a piece of paper and put it in your wallet. Then when you need help, go to churches of that same denomination in the city where you are. Tell the minister, "Pastor so and so of St. Luke's Lutheran Church in my town said that pastors of his denomination are really willing to help kids when they are in trouble. Well, I'm in trouble." Etc., etc.

By the way, and this is not meant to be a slur, kids report to me that it's very difficult to pull this off at Catholic parishes and many Jewish synagogues. If you are going to a Catholic church, look in the yellow pages for one that lists "Franciscan Fathers" or "Paulist Fathers," or a Jewish synagogue labeled "Reform." Your chances will probably be a little better.

Or what if you are looking for a relatively safe place to roll out your sleeping bag for a nice night's snooze? Consider the large metal rubbish containers that are behind the stores at large shopping centers. They are dry, and the noise around them in the morning wakes you up in plenty of time to get out of there. Other places to consider: abandoned railroad cars, culverts, boats that are tied up in such a way indicating that the owners have not been around for a while (especially in winter), and construction shacks that are being stored at the contractor's place of business and are not in use.

If you are out in the country, don't be afraid to ask a farmer if you can roll out your bag in one of his sheds. In fact, when in doubt, it's always a good policy to ask. If you ask in the right way (remember, giving permission to say no), often times you'll score.

Another little thing that you can do that can make it better for other kids who come later is to leave a "blanket of good vibes" when there are other people involved. Clean up, be polite, offer to help with things, etc. If there are no people around, leave a note behind telling how much you enjoyed the spot and how you hope that the place was left in good shape. That note can have real influence over the owner of a construction shed as well as the next person who might sleep there.

Another thing to be really careful of is campfires. If you need to light one to cook or to get warm, do it carefully, put it out carefully. Some people ruined it for a lot of others in Big Sur, California, because they got sloppy about fires, started a few that got away, and made a good number of the local residents hostile to young people who were coming through. These residents loved the area, too, and wanted to protect it.

In terms of just finding food, there are a number of dependable places for coming upon free food. Usually there is discarded food behind most large supermarkets. It's still good, but just not salable by their standards. Mostly you'll find fruit and vegetables, but sometimes there may be canned goods or meat.

Another good place is to look for boarding schools that are in the area. With a little sweet talk you can sometimes get one of the students to invite you as a guest for a meal at the school's dining hall.

Don't be afraid to go to welfare departments, either. Many times the caseworkers there will give you food stamps just to get rid of you. Just start telling your tale of woe in a very long, drawn out, boring way. They'll often interrupt: "What is it you want, a little food? Is that it?"

You respond, "Well, that's not all, but that would sure help me feel a lot better." And you've scored. Sometimes they'll even include a chit for a free night in a not-so-bad hotel.

The men who hang around bus stations, railroad stations, etc., can also give you clues. Don't go with them, though. Just get information about where to go, and go by yourself.

Many communities now have crisis centers for youths, and such centers often have leads on places for free or cheap food and lodging. The Salvation Army is sometimes helpful as well, but usually you'll have to buy into going to a church service or something similar before getting the food or place to sleep that you want. "Jesus People" places are often helpful in this respect. Just be cool, don't put them down for their religious life-style, and they can be quite helpful.

Survival in a strange place or at home can often depend on being able to let it all hang out when things are really getting uptight. Learning how to relax when it's necessary to relax, even when it's almost impossible to do so, is a good skill to master. Because of this, I'd like to suggest a couple of ways that you can develop the art of relaxation.

Depending on where your head is at, you could call what I'm going to suggest self-hypnosis, meditation, relaxation exercises, letting it all hang out, letting go, going with the good vibes — whatever you like to call it. In any event, the label makes no difference. Once you get those "alpha" waves going in your brain, you'll feel your muscles loosen up, your body relax, and you'll be able to sleep easier, study better, and get through uptight situations with much less difficulty. When you learn how to relax, you open up a lot of possibilities.

There are two techniques I am particularly fond of because they are very private, totally something that you do yourself, inside your own reality.

The first one can be done just about anywhere without anyone else knowing what you are doing. You can do it right where you are now. But read through all of the directions before you try. To start, let your body just feel heavy all over. Then focus your eyes on a spot — a picture on the wall, a flower, a burning candle, whatever is available. Try to get a sense of yourself being gathered into that spot which you yourself have choosen.

Next, whenever your own mind allows it to happen, let your eyes close. Just sense how naturally that can happen, without your deciding when they will close. After they close, allow your body to give you a signal through your hands that you have entered into a state of deep relaxation, meditation, whatever you want to call it. Your hand or hands might get warm or cold, tingly, feel light or heavy, your own body will have its own special way of telling you when you've reached that state.

Allow yourself to go with it for as long as you want to. Whenever you want to finish the experience, count to three in your mind, make a fist with your hands, open your hands and open your eyes, and you will continue to feel relaxed and good all over.

A variation which is much more physical and less mental is as follows: Start from the top of your head and then, going down over your entire body, tighten all your muscles and keep them tight until your whole body is just squeezing tighter and tighter. Then, before you relax the tightened muscles, take a very deep breath and hold it about thirty seconds. Now let the breath go, let the muscles go, and just enjoy the waves of relaxation as they flow over your whole body.

One final survival area needs to be touched on, especially because it is one of those areas where people's usual actions get them into more trouble rather than out of trouble. It's those times when you might be in danger of being physically harmed, beaten up, raped, robbed, etc. Everyone has to find his/her own way and adapt a little in these situations; so the following suggestions are made to open up possibilities for you and are not meant to be followed to the letter.

One good rule is never to yell "Help!" If you want to get help, yell "Fire!" and people will come running to see what's going on. Often people will not respond to a call for help because they don't want to "get involved."

If you're in a place where it looks like yelling "fire" will not bring anyone, a good technique is to pretend that you have some strange mental illness. Pretend to be weird or deranged. Don't over-do it, however, or the attackers will know that it's just an act. This is a good technique to practice at home with friends watching so you can know when you have a technique that comes off as being real. Many times, attackers are afraid to attack people who are "different" or "strange" because they do not know what to expect from them.

Surrendering in a dramatic way can often be an effective protec-tion. When someone appraoches who is going to attack, just get real-ly frightened and hysterical in your own way, start breathing very heavily, and then faint, pass out, go absolutely limp. Stay there where you are, don't move, no matter what the attacker does. This is es-pecially helpful if someone should try something in an elevator (which, by the way, is a favorite spot of some rapists and robbers).

If someone comes up from behind and surprises you, just look at the person, gasp for breath, and go limp. Stay limp until you're sure it's safe to move. When you go limp, try to land on your side or stomach so it will be more dificuly for the attacker to tell whether you're in bad shape. The position will also afford you more pro-tection.

If the attacker is a lone male and you are caught in a struggle be-fore you have been able to use any of the suggestions we've men-tioned, consider a very hard kick or knee into his groin. If you can get hold of them, grab his testicles, pull straight down, and twist hard. Either of these tactics will effectively immobilize him while you get away. But if you try these, don't go easy. Do it really hard or it might backfire.

If the attacker is a woman, one of the most vulnerable places is the bridge of the nose, right between the eyes. But don't play. It's better not to solve these things physically, but if that's what you are forced into doing, do it hard.

As a general rule, whenever it's possible, don't walk alone. Try to be with someone, even if it's someone you don't know that you decide to stay close to. Most attacks happen when people are alone. Attackers are usually cowards.

Again, it is generally better to "go with something" than to fight it. It's just amazing how often a rapist will be thrown off balance if the woman when approached by him says, "Well, it looks like it's going to happen, I might as well surrender. Would you give me a little time to take my clothes off and get ready?" The rapist is looking for fear. That's part of the excitement that he gets out of the experience. The reaction described above takes that payoff away from him and often the rapist loses the desire and runs off, of it can put him off enough to give you time to run away. It's really hard to keep your cool in that way in a situation like this, but it can really pay off.

Another example of this same principle: A woman who had taken a course from me was in a park. A "Lily Waver" came up to her. That's a man who likes to show his penis in public to girls or women. Well, he unzipped his fly, pulled it out to wave at her. She looked calmly at him and then said, "Gee, I feel so sorry for you." With which the man hung his head and ran off into the bushes. I think she not only helped herself, but she probably made the man think twice about whether he'd "wave his lily" at any other women.

When things get just a little out of balance, a little off the way people expect things to go, it's very difficult for them to keep on doing what they had planned to do. With a little practice, you can develop this ability to do the unexpected which lies somewhere vaguely between the either/or.

Let me close with one personal example. I was once called to help some speed freaks who were in trouble in their apartment. When I got there I found to my dismay that they had decided that I was "the man" — a policeman — and were waiting to really work me over. Well, there were about a dozen of them and my immediate reaction was, "I can *either* fight with them *or* I can try to run away." But because of experience and practice, my head said, "Either of those actions is going to get wiped out." So I lay down on the floor in front of them with my arms outstretched and said, "Well, if you're going to do it you'd better start, 'cause there's no way I'm any match for all of you." The room got deathly silent, people mumbled a little, and quickly went streaming out the door, leaving me lying there alone. Now I don't know what they decided or what they said, but I do know they didn't work me over. And that's another victory for uncommon sense.

Remember, when we're in trouble, common sense very often makes things worse. Practice developing skills in which your own uncommon sense becomes natural.

Chapter 5
CHOICES

Propositions: Being adult doesn't mean that you are wise, noble, or good. It means, in large part, that you make your own choices. In fact, as an adult, you don't have an alternative — *you HAVE to make your own choices.*

One way to let people know that you are really on top of things is to make your own choices. When you are in your teens, of course, there are certain choices you're not allowed to make. For instance, you might not have any choice regarding where you live, where you go to school, or what kind of meals you eat. These choices, generally are made by your parents.

On the other hand, by the time you are in high school you may be choosing most of your clothing, deciding what courses to take in school, and deciding what you do for recreation.

The ability to make choices — particularly the ability to make good choices — doesn't come to you (or anybody) by magic; it's something you have to learn. And most people learn by the trial and error method. The sooner you learn to make good choices, the sooner you have control of your life. Unfortunately, when you're young, there are all sorts of people who won't allow you to make choices. They could be your parents, your teachers, or any people who are in a position of power over you. They will often make choices for you because they believe you are not capable of making good choices.

Let's assume that the choices they make for you are good ones (which isn't necessarily true); you still lose, because you haven't learned anything in the process. Presumably they want to help you to learn to be an adult, but actually they hurt you, for not only are you denied the right to make the choices adults make, you also get the message that you don't have the ability to make choices. In other words, you are still a child who must be told what to do.

A lot of the conflicts that occur between parents and their children concern this business of choices. It's essentially a matter of who has the power. The way you evolve from being a dependent child to being a free adult depends on how you take this power away from your parents. There are at least three ways you can do this:

1. *Remove them from power.* This is a pretty radical method. You might try kicking them out of the house, but they might not be willing to leave, particularly if they are the ones paying the rent. Exile and deportation are possibilities, but there's an awful lot of paper work involved.

2. *Remove yourself from their control.* This, too, is a pretty radical method, but worth considering. As a matter of fact, I doubt there is anyone over the age of three who hasn't considered running away from home at one time or another. And remember, "runaway" is not a naughty word. After all, history is filled with people who ran away from impossible situations and found opportunities for better lives. (See vignette about runaways).

3. *The Godfather method.* Make them an offer they can't refuse.

Let's talk about method three. What you do with this method is to present choices of your own to your parents that are as good as, or even better than, any they could come up with. Unless they are being really blockheaded (and parents often are like that) they have to go along with you. It's to their advantage because they're spared the trouble of deciding for you. And as you begin to make your own good choices, your parents have to recognize your capabilities.

If you are presently making most of the choices that affect your life, you probably don't have to worry very much about a strategy for gaining power. If, however, you feel you are too much under your parents' control, you should start doing something about it.

How to begin? Start at the beginning. If the first suggestion in your campaign for power is that your parents sell the house and move to a commune, you'll probably find you've given them an offer they can very easily refuse. Make *two* suggestions like that, and they probably won't allow you to choose your own socks until you're drawing Social Security.

But say, for instance, your parents have always made the choice of what the family is going to have for dinner. Here's an area where you can make an inroad. Tell them that you want to cook dinner on a particular night and ask if they'd be willing to go along with your choice of food. It's a suggestion they'll probably consider because it offers them something. It offers them free time they otherwise would have to spend preparing the meal.

It's not likely you can offer your parents financial advantages, but you can offer to give them free time. And free time is an offer few people would refuse. Free time, in fact, is the basic commodity you use in trading for power with your parents. It's a nice kind of trading because both parties gain freedom — you are free to make choices, they are free from the obligation to supervise everything you do.

The act of choosing is, in itself, important because that's how you learn to make choices. Beyond that is the matter of what you make choices about. Most people would agree that choosing whether or not they drop out of school is a more important decision than choosing what brand of mustard the family brings to a barbeque.

As you acquire the power to make more choices, you'll probably also want to be making more important choices. Choices that are often made by your parents — at a time when you are making most of the decisions about your personal life — are the choices of what doctor, dentist, lawyer (if you're in trouble with the law) or psychiatrist you go to. It may be that your parents know more about such things than you; however, there may be times when you need help that you would prefer to choose the person who is going to help you.

If you need medical help, there are definite advantages in seeing your family doctor. For one thing, your parents will probably pay the fees for you and they'll feel comfortable knowing that you're in the care of someone they trust. There's also the advantage that your family doctor has your medical history since you were a child and knows about any problems that have developed along the way. A lot of red tape involving medical history, family background, etc., can be eliminated. And, of course, you might like the doctor yourself.

If your problems are something you want to keep confidential, you might not feel secure going to your family doctor. You might feel that she would discuss the situation with your parents. Maybe she would and maybe she wouldn't, but if there is any question about that, it could be a problem.

Some problems could arise if you are seeking information regarding birth control, if you have an unwanted pregnancy or if you've contracted a veneral disease. In any of these instances, you might not feel comfortable with your family doctor.

On the other hand, if you want a way to get information to your family — a controlled leak, as they say in Washington — your family doctor might be just the person to help you.

For instance, you might be able to arrange with the family doctor that he should tell your parents that you have an unwanted pregnancy and that you want to deal with it. Depending on what your relationship with your parents is, it could be less of a blow to them to have the information channeled through a professional person such as the family doctor.

You can do that sort of thing right out front — just make a straight bargain with him — or you might tell him that you have a problem and it's up to him whether or not he wants to talk about it with your parents. Either way, the family doctor can be a good communication bridge between you and your parents.

Even with a good family doctor, you still might want to have your own doctor, one to whom you can talk about personal problems without worrying if he'll keep the information confidential. Another reason for choosing your own doctor is to show your parents that you're changing — that you're taking care of yourself and learning to make important choices on your own. If you present the situation to your parents that way, your choice of your own doctor isn't a rejection of the family doctor.

A good way to start looking for your own doctor is to check with your friends. Ask them if they've found a doctor they think is reliable. If you've got older friends, ones who've had a little more experience than you, their opinion could be valuable.

You could also check with a youth crisis center in your community, such as a drug abuse center. Such places often have a list of doctors who are reliable in working with young people, who will keep confidences, who know their business, and who are in close touch with the problems that young people have.

Finally, if you live in a small community where you don't have such centers, there are other ways you can check out a doctor. A good way is to set up an appointment with a doctor when you don't actually have anything wrong.

Since you'll probably be paying the bills, check to see how much the first visit is going to cost. If it seems unreasonable, explain that you aren't in a position to pay that much. But be sure that it *is* unreasonable. If the price is too high for your pocketbook, you can ask the receptionist if the doctor could give you a lower rate for the first visit. If he won't, just cross him off your list. But if it is a reasonable amount, go and pay it. It's well worth the investment to find out if you can trust the doctor. You will have to decide what is a reasonable amount. Basically, it's what you can afford.

It's important to find out from your parents if you can have the privilege of having your own health insurance card that you can use with any doctor you choose. Your parents may have health insurance from the place where they work and may be able to get you your own card for use with a doctor of your choice. You should determine before you go to the doctor whether you want to tell him that you have health insurance because part of your first visit will involve filling out a form that will probably ask if you have health insurance. There will probably be a release for you to sign indicating that the doctor has permission to obtain your health records from any other doctor you've seen. That doesn't mean he's trying to pry into your affairs, it's the normal way doctors' offices operate.

When you get to the doctor's office, pay close attention to how the receptionist treats you. That's important because you can tell a lot about the doctor by the way the receptionist is trained and acts.

Before your examination begins there are things you should be on the lookout for. Does the receptionist make you feel at home? How long does the doctor make you wait? Do the doctor and his staff treat you as a person of value? Do they treat you as an adult, or do they talk down to you?

When you get in with the doctor, you can have him examine you for almost anything — you don't have to go to the expense of a full medical examination. Remember though, right from the beginning you should let the doctor know that you're really interested in taking care of yourself, and that it's important to you that your parents don't know that you're coming to see him. See how he reacts and decide for yourself how trustworthy you think he is.

You can test him in various ways. For instance, if you're a young man, ask him if he'd be willing to talk to you about venereal disease or drugs and give you help in those areas. If you're a young woman, you could ask if he'd be willing to help you with an unwanted pregnancy.

The important thing isn't whether he says he'll help you, but the way in which he responds to you. Does he respond in a way that shows he'll be willing to keep your confidences? Does he show a willingness to help you meet your needs, even if he can't meet them himself? Is he willing to take the time to answer your questions and give you detailed explanations? If you're a woman, try to find out how sensitive you doctor is to your womanhood. Some doctors (both male and female) take the attitude that their female patients are usually not genuinely in need of medical help but are just chronic complainers. It's also very important to notice whether the doctor treats you as though you are a human being and not just some smart aleck kid.

There's no surefire method of knowing what kind of person a new doctor is, but using your own sensitivity, you can probably get a pretty good reading. If you've given the doctor an initial once-over and you're still not sure how reliable he is, you can proble a little deeper. Try telling him something about yourself that might sound a little far out — something that some doctors might feel they had to tell your parents — and then stop before you've finished. For instance, you could say, "You know, I've been having some problems, but I don't know if I should talk about them now — maybe I should wait for another time." Then see how he responds.

If he's willing to allow you the dignity of keeping your affairs private, that's probably a good sign. If, however, he tries to milk the information out of you, that's probably a dangerous sign. And if he calls your parents later, that's a dangerous sign for sure, and he's definitely not the sort of doctor you're looking for.

If you know any nurses, aides, or orderlies who work at a local hospital, you could ask them to recommend a doctor. They often know from firsthand experience that the smiling "Marcus Welby" is actually an insensitive bully. On the other hand, they can often tell you which doctors practice good medicine and have a genuine concern for other human beings.

The methods for checking out a doctor's reliability can be used to check out the reliability of other people in the helping professions. It's probably worth the effort to check out your school counselor because not all school counselors are trustworthy. Some of them are more interested in saving their own necks than in helping young people.

One way to do it is with a phoney issue, similar to the one suggested for checking out doctors. You could make up something that you wouldn't want the counselor to tell your parents and then see whether he protects your confidentiality or his neck.

Another way of checking out people who are supposed to be helping you is to ask them if they have a number where you can reach them in off-duty hours. It's a pretty good barometer of a person's reliability if she is available during nonbusiness hours, of if she has someone covering for her who could help in her absence. This is especially true for school counselors.

I would say that any school counselor who won't give you his home phone number is probably not a good one to go to with your problems. That's not true for all professionals, but I'd say that a teacher or counselor who won't give you a home phone number is probably not reliable, though there can be exceptions.

For example, a counselor or teacher might have someone at home who is seriously ill and wouldn't want phone calls coming to his home because it would upset the sick person. Or a counselor or teacher may have been the victim of crank calls and wants to take his phone number out of circulation for awhile.

But generally speaking, someone who's genuinely interested in helping young people is willing to give out his number because that sort of person doesn't generally get abused by young people. They don't usually get called in the middle of the night unless it's really important.

That's another thing to remember — if you have someone who's willing to help you with your problems, don't call him at odd hours if it can wait until the next day. Don't call just because you're hurting; call only when you really need to make that call.

If you have the misfortune to be involved in a criminal case, a public defender is probably the best lawyer you can get — assuming you haven't the money to hire F. Lee Bailey or Perry Mason — because he constantly deals with criminal law. Ordinary lawyers aren't that accustomed to dealing with criminal law because they deal with civil cases, business transactions, divorces, etc.

Most of the time — unless the public defender's office in your community is very bad — the public defender will be the best person to handle your case, especially if you take the time to get with him and talk about the case and insist on a little service from him. Most of the time, public defenders are so busy they don't have time to deal with your case until just before you walk into the courtroom. But if you take the time to make appointments to talk about the case and take the opportunity to get him interested in your situation, he'll probably produce for you.

But again — test him out. Find out from people your own age, if possible, who the good defenders are, who the reliable ones are. As you talk with him, see how he relates to you as a person, in much the same way as I suggested you do with a doctor. You can tell a lot by the way the receptionists handle you, how the lawyers will handle you because if the lawyers care about those things, they'll train their employees to deal with you in appropriate ways.

Sometimes a public defender (or any lawyer) might try to persuade you to "cop a plea" for a small sentence. We feel that if a lawyer is trying to do anything other than keep you out of jail, it's a danger sign.

If he says you should "cop a plea" for a suspended sentence, but no actual time in juvenile hall, reform school, detention hall, honor camp, rehabilitation center (or whatever the authorities in your area call their kids' prisons), that's probably a good sign. However, if the lawyers say you should take a small sentence in kids' prison, that's probably a bad sign.

With lawyers, reputation is very important. People at a youth crisis center might be good ones to talk to about getting a lawyer, but even then it's important that you talk to the lawyer yourself and try to get a feeling of how he'll handle your case. Ask him if he's had similar cases and ask how he handled them. And find out what happened to the clients in those cases. If the outcome was something you could accept in your case, he might be the lawyer for you.

If you find yourself in a bind where the courts, your parents, or you, yourself, decide you should get "psychiatric help," a pretty good general rule is to avoid psychiatrists. They are the "shrinks" with M.D. after their names. They're generally trained to take the approach that a person has something wrong inside of him that needs to be corrected rather than seeing their task as helping a person learn the skill necessary to deal with the problem. Also, many rely on mind-controlling drugs to alter their clients' behavior. There are, of course, exceptions to the rule. If you have advice from a trustworthy friend that such and such a psychiatrist is all right, then it might be worth talking with him.

I feel, though, that you'll have better luck if you look for someone with the label "family therapist," "counselor," "social worker" or "psychologist."

There are a number of free health services available. We've mentioned youth crisis centers. There are also a number of free clinics in many communities, including public health clinics. But you shouldn't be surprised if a public health clinic charges you for its services because a lot of public agencies do charge according to the client's income. If you have no income, they might try to have your parents pay. And that's why it's important to find out at the beginning how to deal with the agencies. You should know from the start whether or not they are willing to deal with you on the basis of who you are without relationship to who your parents are.

If you're really low on money and find you can't get free professional help — be it legal, medical, or help in solving problems — you may be able to work out an installment payment plan with the helping person. When you see the person initially, you should ask if payments can be spread out. Not only will that take a load off your mind (and pocketbook), you'll be able to determine whether the person understands the financial problems of young people. If he does, that's an indication that he might also be tuned into other problems of young people.

Chapter 6
A PERSONAL ACCOUNT

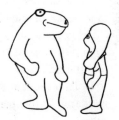

by Cheryl Arnold

In my life I've chosen not to have children. And I've decided with my husband to be married for only one year at a time. Looking around me and not seeing many others making these kinds of choices, I know I've had to be somewhat stubborn, certain, and alone to come to them myself. I feel right, that I've done the right thing for myself, so far, in this time, in this place. But I'd feel wrong if I got into persuading you to think like me.

After all, it's no distinction to be right. That's where each of us is coming from. If I try to wipe out your rightness, I'm losing hold of mine. The only way I can talk about these things is personally: by showing here's what's happened to me, and what I've made to happen for me. Maybe something in it will connect with you; that's what I'd like to happen.

What it's all about for me is each person getting a chance to make his/her own life.

Where to start? Maybe in the middle . . . A few years ago I was growing very close to a man named John. We hadn't talked about marriage, but we were wanting more and more to be together. And we'd had enough highs and lows and time together to see that reality seemed to be deepening our love, not rubbing out our romance.

We'd talked enough about other people's marriages to know that neither of us was eager to marry, even for love. We hadn't talked about just living together, maybe because such a decision would create a scandal in that time and that place and that would have cut us off from most of the important people in our lives.

One day, when John was moderating a radio talk show, I tuned in to hear him discussing thoughts on marriage. I found myself listening closely to ideas I hadn't heard him express before. "Ten years from now, the institution of marriage will have expanded into a lot of different forms . . . . People will make special marriage agreements to fit their needs and desires . . . . The law will provide for short-term marriages, so people can change partners without devastating each other . . . "

I guess this must have rolled around in the back of my head because some days later while we ate in a restaurant I said to John, "You know what you were saying on the radio about marriage — like how ten years from now it will be different? Well, why couldn't it start being different now? Why couldn't people just decide to make their own kind of marriage, even if the law hasn't said it's OK yet?"

John's eyes twinkled as he replied, "What are you saying, Cheryl?"

Because I hadn't said, "Why couldn't *we*" — for I was much too shy to say that.

At that point we started talking together about this exciting idea — if we could design our own marriage relationship, how would we go about it? Just the daring, and going through the talking were so important. We were learning to speak of heavy things without laying heavy trips on each other. And the intimacy drew us into a growing respect and commitment.

We came up with a contract, in which we agreed to allow each other our own names, not to have children, how we'd divide property if the marriage ended, etc., for an initial period of two years. Two lawyer friends helped us put it in legal language, and when we were married, we filed the contract with the County Clerk as an addendum to the standard marriage certificate.

Going Through Changes in an Old and New World

This rather bold behavior came seven years and 2,000 miles away from my Middle America upbringing, and probably couldn't have happened there. Yet, as with all of us, what we have done is a part of what we do next; and I feel I have remained true to much that I was taught to value then. In that pioneer place we learned to value individuality, but that was not to be confused with being different. We were expected to be honest, but not about everything. As a girl, I was rewarded by adults for doing well in school, but snubbed by many kids for the same behavior. There were "no-no's" beneath every surface. Maybe I was unusually sensitive, but it seemed to me that most of us there stayed wrapped in our invisible shields. We didn't touch each other much, but we exerted powerful holds on one another.

Now, I think that kind of life is OK if people choose it, but, like any child, I hadn't been given a choice. Eventually I needed to get some space and time away before I could even see and hear and feel myself — get a sense of who I was and what I wanted to do.

I've always thought it strange and kind of awful how human beings can keep their children being children for so long. The way we have it set up, "kids" are living in their parents' homes and going to school at age 18, much as they did at age 6; and it's hard for most people to change a relationship like that, that's just kept on going. Even the parents who tell their 16-year-olds that they "must learn to be responsible" are still telling their children what they must do.

This can be awfully frustrating. I can see why some people get married first chance they get; maybe they've felt ready to be an adult for a long time. But it makes me sad to see a man or woman who's never had a chance to be out there on his/her own, never had a chance to be crazy, to make mistakes without hurting anybody, to find out how many kinds of amazing people there are in this world. You don't get these chances if you move straight from being a child to being a parent — and it's sure not the same thing to be "free" after your marriage has fallen apart and you've your own kids depending on you till they're 18.

The way I started learning about love and intimacy and getting along and breaking through games with people was by doing it — which included some danger, some crying, some foolishness, some loving more than I was loved in return, some hurting and getting hurt, some feeling older and wiser, but nothing I'm ashamed of, because I was out there getting it together with life, and there wasn't much I could hurt other than myself.

It's pretty hard to learn anything if you're not allowed to make mistakes. In the old days, the only way a woman and man found out if they could make it together was by getting married. I wonder how many of them knew, just one week later, that they'd made a mistake. But they weren't allowed to make mistakes. They weren't allowed to get divorced. However, they had one important thing over us: in the old days, most people didn't *expect* marriage to be romantic or smooth or happy. They were *lucky* if it worked out that way for them.

From what I've heard about the "old days" (they really weren't that long ago), a lot of things were different. Romance was less important then because there was so much work to do. When people got married, they took on a big job. Childhood and play were pretty much over. And once people had children, they spent the rest of their lives caring for the family. People didn't do much changing, and neither did the world. People lived in one place and did the same work all their lives; everybody in the family worked hard just to survive. Of course, they died earlier, too. Parents would die before all the kids were out of the house, and lots of husbands and wives didn't have time to get tired of each other.

All that business about brideprice and the men doing some fancy trading over women's bodies is reprehensible to me now, but I can see a little how it fitted into the old economics. While men treated women as inferior beings and everything was judged from a male standard, women had clear economic values, just as men did. For example, a woman with wide hips looked like she'd bear a lot of strong children, who would then work and help bring prosperity to the family. And I suppose the main reason women's work was raising the children and doing all the work around the household (heavy work in those days!) was that a good share of the time they were pregnant or nursing babies.

This sounds like the Dark Ages to most of us, but I think a lot of it is still around. Like the crude jokes that still go on about how a man is giving up his freedom when he gets married. Like the reverse assumption for women: she has reached her highest goal in life, catching her man, and now she can relax and let life run its course with her. Like most people believing that a woman *must* give up her name at marriage. Like newspapers still referring to women as Mrs. John Taylor, and even when they write about Margaret Thatcher, telling you what she wore.

Like how in many states a husband has to take full financial responsibility, and a wife is treated like her husband's child. Like, when I am writing this, the lawmakers of this country are still struggling over the question as to whether women are as full human beings as men. Like how many women still promise to "honor and obey" their husbands. Like how in some states a woman and her children cannot get the welfare money they have already qualified for if a man is living in the house (because the man secretly is or should be supporting the household, even if he has no legal responsibility).

Like how men can't get "women's jobs" and women can't "men's jobs." Like some recent statistics: in the U.S., women were 40 percent of the work force; even women with children were working outside the home and had been doing so for 20 to 25 years; yet women's wages were 41 percent less than men's. Like how when many adults meet someone new, they look for a wedding ring; its presence or absence will determine how they relate to that person. Like how when a couple goes out socially, the man is asked, "What do you do?" and the woman is asked, "Do you have children?"

Our society is sometimes old and sometimes new. And many of us are cruelly treated if we believe one "truth" society tells us — the next day we might be told that the opposite is equally true. A little girl can grow up thinking that marriage will be bliss with her husband and children; after she's gotten into it, she finds out the family won't make it unless she works both outside and inside the home. A woman can devote 30 years of her life to her family and be proud and fulfilled in a job well done. Then society's values shift and the woman gets the message that she hasn't done enough; she's been conned into a lifetime of mindless, unimportant work. Or a woman may have several years of the traditional arrangement. One day she wakes up with three kids and mortgages and a lot of people expecting her to do a lot of hard, unrewarded work. She looks at TV, magazines, other people — and she wants more out of life, but it's too late. She has no way out, no way to make it on her own.

For a man, the usual variation on this theme is that he wakes up one morning the same way, feeling trapped, and TV and advertising messages have made him especially afraid about losing his youth. At about the same time he meets a young woman who may have been treated like a feather-headed sex object by the young men who have courted her. The younger woman and older man are just right for each other; society has programmed them that way. Then society usually programs that the marriage breaks up, and the wife stays with the children. In most cases like this, you can't point a finger at the man or woman and say who is to blame. It's a combination of what they've done together, and a lot more of what society has done to them.

Our society is going through lots of necessary changes right now, and the word is out that it's necessary for people to change. When I look at broken marriages of people I know, it seems that many of them are cases of people wanting to change but their relationships were not being strong enough to change. Our society doesn't train us well in how to have close relationships, how to go through rough times together, how to forgive. If you're going to live a long time with somebody, some times will be great, some will be dull, some will be troubled, etc. That's life. But our society trains us to be dissatisfied if things aren't always great. There are always so many new and exciting things we can do and have in life.

Up Against It

Although I was nearly 28 years old when John and I started thinking about marriage, I was still afraid of it. There I was, in the most beautiful time of my life, and I was afraid that marriage would ruin it. We knew a couple who had lived together for seven years; they got married and were separated within four months. Marriage would change our relationship, for sure, and I feared that we would get closed down, rather than opened up. Because the greatest thing — my love for John — had not brought my life to a focus on him; no, it had opened up my life to more people and less fear.

For myself, I expected people would start treating me as Mrs. John.

I wouldn't be me anymore. Men who had always been pleasant to me wouldn't waste compliments on me anymore. Overnight, people would put me in a married woman's bag — and that wasn't my bag! But you can't tell people how to treat you, especially when they're treating you like you're someone else. Like many women I knew, I might grow resentful and need to lash out, probably at John instead of at the real culprits, just recause he was close at hand and maybe the only person to whom I would dare express anger.

All around us, the divorce rate was escalating. Divorces were like family wars, with children and property being used as weapons. I figured that some of these divorced people must have started out with a terrific relationship like we had, so why should we be safe from all the forces that bring people to divorce? As for John, he felt pretty much the same way about the whole subject, and with some reason — he himself had already been married and divorced!

Luckily, we didn't give in to this gloom and doom. We decided not to be victims, but rather to take charge and get those good things working for us. We talked about what was precious to us, how we could protect and nurture these things. We talked about why we wanted to live together, the dreams that would then be possible. We talked about the things we didn't want to happen (like possessiveness, dependency, jealousy), and how, just maybe, we could engineer them out.

What we came up with, our contract, has been very good for us. Of course, it was just the beginning of a process that has grown for 14 years now. Where I had feared doldrums and dependency, we now have greater happiness and less dependency than when we began. And I can see that we're not holding each other down when I realize how much each of us has changed during these years.

All of this is not to say that anyone else should do it our way. The whole point for us is that any couple has a unique, personal relationship. Marriage should be set up to foster that specialness, rather than force everyone into the same mold. Even if a man and a woman say to each other, "We want to be married till death do us part," and the woman will wear a long white dress and promise to obey, and the man will earn the money and make the big decisions, and the woman will work at home and raise many children — how different that relationship is from one where people just walk through the same trip unconsciously, never considering if it's what they really want.

Some people say our marriage contract sounds "negative." Maybe that's because we've been so sure about what we do *not* want. But I'll shout-whisper-sing-say that it's the most positive thing I've ever done. To speak of love can *add* intimacy to a kiss. To want a love that honors and sets free — that's positive. To hear the world say, "No, you can't do that," and to answer, "Yes, we certainly can"; to hang onto someone for just a year at a time — I think that shows confidence. And how many people are lucky enough to hear, at least once a year, "Yes, I want to be married to you!" That's how we're doing it now: once a year we go off somewhere together, so we can free our minds and focus on what's happening with us. Sometimes we revise our contract. Sometimes we just renew it. We figure that to make it new each year is more positive for us than anniversaries, and, besides, it's a great occasion for a party.

To Be or Not to Be a Parent

I suppose someone who has read this far might think, "Well, of course, anyone who's as selfish and scared of dependency as she is wouldn't want to have children."

It's true; I am selfish. There are many things I like to do that I don't think I could manage if I had to be a mother, too. Maybe some day our society will work it out so that kids can get all the love and care they need without parents having to put so much energy in that direction. (Wealthy people seem to manage better these days.) Maybe I'll change, too, and some day want to take on that responsibility. I know that tomorrow, if some child needed a home and I seemed the right one to provide, I would do it. Even now, I enjoy the fun of caring for children in that special way when John's three children live with us on weekends and vacations. But if we are to have any choices in life, I think men and women should have a free choice whether or not to take on an 18-year-or-more responsibility for another person's life.

As it is, having a child is just about the longest and fullest commitment a person can make — a much heavier commitment than marriage. Men and women can "change their minds" after marriage. A woman can't change her mind after having a child. Unfortunately, our society still allows men to walk away. I read in the newspaper recently that within only one year of divorce, more than 40 percent of the fathers are not paying their share of child support. If a couple is thinking about having children, they have to think about "we," but each person also has to think about "I."

I love the special ways of children, which is one reason I became an elementary school teacher. For me, it can be deadly to be with just adults all the time. Kids give out lots of energy, and they take a lot, too, which is why I have come home worn-out after a day of teaching school.

If I ever decide to raise a child, it will not be to have one that is "mine" — I don't want to own anybody, and I haven't met many people who want to be owned. Nor do I want to put a child in the bind of being the person who provides the glue in my life.

Part of the trouble for me is that I go overboard the other way. I so much want people to be free. Kids don't have much freedom — they have to take what's given them. And so if I had kids, I'd work on giving them chances to meet life in a variety of ways; I wouldn't want to just "lay my trip on them." Even to be a fair and generous and intelligent and nice parent isn't enough, in my book, because I might be sending out too strong a message: "Be like me." Maybe, for example, if a child has the room to experiment a little with stinginess, he/she will decide that generosity is a happier way.

If I ever decide to raise a child, it must be for the joy and pleasure of sharing life with a person in this tremendously involving way. I'll have to want that joy and pleasure so much that I'll be willing to put my body through some heavy changes — sacrifice precious times of privacy — arrange my daily life, work and earning possibilities, travel, education, sleeping, eating, spending, social life, sex life, vacations, place and type of home, and a few other things around the needs of the child — take special care that I do not become primarily a "Mother" rather than a "Wife - Lover - Parent" together with my husband — after I've given and given and given, know that I cannot demand that love be returned — after I've involved myself in years of caring for this dependent person, know that he/she might just move out of my life, might even hurt me in pulling loose, whether I'm ready for that or not.

This business of being free — to me it doesn't mean independence from other people. One of the things I want most in life is relationships with other people. But, as I said, I want relationships that open up life, rather than close it down.

And for me, that's really what's happening.

Chapter 7
RELIGION – IS IT EVEN WORTH TALKING ABOUT?

Maybe not — maybe religion is such a small force for so few people that it isn't even worth discussing anymore. And yet there seem to be so many religious things happening these days. There are Jesus Freaks and Catholics and Moonies and Hassidics and TMers and Hare Krishnas and Buddhists and Lutherans and Baptists and Satanists and TAers and 3 HOers and CPers and Primalers and, and — so many pressures and forces around that are RELIGION.

For me, I'm fed up with "religious" people — they're, at least to me, a drag. They are people who have a one-track mind, want everyone to have their particular form of faith. They have all the answers, know just what you should do, I should do, the whole world should do. Nice neat packages, "do this," mostly, "don't do that," a sickening lot. Now, that's my opinion. What follows is my point of view about these things — you might not agree at all.

In this age when so many things are being sold as answers to everything (some might accuse me of doing just that in this book), maybe it is important to spend a little time talking about religion. It can't be all bad, can it?

Certainly Nixon and company had "religion" — for them, their approach was so "right" (correct) that it allowed them to force their rightness on others through methods "wrong" in any other book. It was a religion that clearly said, "We know what is right for us, and for you too and if you don't agree, something must be wrong with you!" The whole episode reminded me of what the Roman Emperor did to the Christians, feeding them to the lions; or what the Inquisitors did, for the church and religion, burning witches at the stake; and what so many religious people have done persecuting Jews, or Blacks, or Arabs, or _____.

Today's type of religious people can persecute even their own kind, Christians against Christians, for example: "If you don't have the baptism of the Holy Ghost, you don't really have faith." Have you had anyone tell you that? I have.

Or have you been confronted by any "converters" — those who run around asking people if they have been saved, seen the light, learned to know Gogah? (She's a new one. Funny how few god-figures are women, except for the one I just made up. Any ideas why?) Have you ever considered how they would feel if *everyone* were converted to their cause, their god? I have a feeling they would be disappointed, helpless, no longer having a cause.

It always amazes me when anyone dares to interpret for the universe *exactly* what God means or is. These very bold people are often afraid of others who are "different." They seem to have the same basic insecurity, fear of life, as the ancient monk, Simeon Stilites, who sat on top of a pole for most of his life.

Then there are those for whom religion can be a powerful cop-out, much like drugs, a notion that one has reached a different state of consciousness. "Hey, I get so far out meditating on Betabubel, I don't need drugs." Or, "Now that I'm part of the fellowship, I'm happy all the time! What a trip!"

Of course, heroin is used toward the same end, but I don't believe it is in the nature of things for people to be happy *all* the time. Fullness of life to me is experiencing all things possible for a human being, and being safe experiencing them. It's important to experience grief and joy, sadness and exhilaration, low points and high points — the breadth of what it is to be human. To be stuck in *one* place is, in my opinion, to be less than human.

Some people discover that religion is an effective way to rebel — again, similar to drugs. If your family is Jewish, you can cause an awful lot of trouble becoming a Jesus Freak — you can command your parents' attention. Or vice versa. Parents can find themselves in a difficult bind if their child does something good (goes to church) in a way that is troublesome (holier-than-thou conversion).

Let me be clear. I'm not talking about situations where people really change their direction, become new and better persons, working for good, changing the world. Rather, I'm talking about situations where there is trouble between people, and religion is used as a weapon in the conflict. Parents often do this with children as well, trying to use religion, maybe a minister, priest or rabbi, to make their children behave, lay guilt trips on them, etc.

So how do I put it all together? I'm not fed up with people who have faith, an inner force that motivates them for good. To me, that's different from being "religious." I think there are some clear signs that show the difference between those who are "religious" and those who have an "inner force" type of faith.

1. They are not out trying to convert the world. They have something that is good for them, but they don't need to lay it on others. Others may be drawn to them and their organizations by the quality of life they exhibit, an impression they give of being together, caring for each other. (By the way, that's the literal meaning of the word salvation – being "whole" or "together" – in the Hebrew root of the word.)

2. Their lives are marked not so much by what they want to get out of their faith as how much they want to do for others because of their faith. They are out working for justice for all under the law; out trying to eliminate the causes of poverty and disease in the world; out helping their neighbor who is in trouble. The key word is OUT, that their "inner force" propels them OUT into a concern for others. Not that I think everyone should be out changing the world either. There is a real place for a "quiet faith." But "a private faith" also makes a difference to others. It can affect an attitude of caring for others, even when they have no inkling of personal faith being the motivating force.

3. They are open to criticism. They don't pretend to have it all nailed down tight in a neat little box. They listen to others, give and take in dialogue, without needing to convice others of their rightness. They have firm personal convictions, without needing to put others down.

Now you may agree with me, or you may wildly disagree. It's hard to talk about personal beliefs in a general way. I happen to be a Lutheran minister — the Christian faith that is part of my tradition is important to me. But you have a way that may be important to you. There are many different "ways" in which people work out the forces and beliefs that motivate them. I would not say that my way is the best for everyone, but I do think that it is the best for me, and I hope it is beneficial to my attitude and behavior toward others.

In any event, religion is an issue that is hard to avoid for people growing up today. It's a very current "hassle." It is part of a continuously battering stream of stimulation we get from our massive society, and it can affect our lives powerfully — even if it's somebody else's religion, such as friends' or parents'. Thus, religion is worth making decisions about, rather than just taking a ride on what's passing through that day. Decisions about religion can be helped by "action plans," "doing plans," just as any other areas of life.

We all have things we "believe in." These beliefs are strong influences on the rest of our lives, whether we believe that there is no god, or that there is one god whose name is Betabubel. Maybe, just maybe, this small chapter about religion (the shortest in the book) has helped you toward some new thoughts about your own beliefs.

Chapter 8
LOVE THY NEIGHBOR – NO WAY

My wife was driving from San Francisco to Carmel on a lonely stretch of Highway 101 at night. She is fair and blonde. Sitting beside her was a friend, Lance, who is black. As they rode, two white males in a '57 Chevy began to harass them, pulling alongside and yelling obscene taunts, trying to make them leave the road. The two young whites in the car were angry to think that one of "them" had one of "theirs."

This is one example of an incident where people cannot be indifferent about race. My wife and Lance had to deal with the situation. Luckily, they spotted "Highway Patrol, Next Right," turned off, and lost their pursuers. But the story might not have ended so neatly.

You're Chicano. You bring home your new girl friend to meet the family. She's Anglo. Your father's a proud man, doesn't think he has prejudices, but he doesn't know how to relate to this situation, doesn't have the experience. The atmosphere is tense. Your girl friend doesn't know what to do either, but wants him to like her. She thinks that showing you affection, a hug, a kiss on the cheek, will let him know how much she cares for you.

There we are again – trouble. An incident, a situation where a person *has to* do something, has to react.

I could go on and on with illustrations. Different groups, different races, different clubs, different activities, different identities. Hells Angels, Gypsy Jokers, Blacks, Whites, Yellows, Reds, Browns, Native Americans, Swedes, Italians, Germans, Finns, Poles, Thai,

59

Russians, Chinese, Brazilians, Yugoslavians, Aussie, upper class, working class, lower class — different ways that people divide themselves or are divided by others.

"This school is prejudiced — all the _____ teachers are in one part of the building, and that means our rights are not protected."

Most of the time, such accusations contain at least one part truth. The cork blows, people are polarized, every attempt at solution seems to make things worse. People become more and more convinced of whom they don't like, of who must change and what must change. "You are a racist." "I am not, this is a case of reverse racism." Ping, pong, on and on.

As with other difficult problems, well-meaning efforts to solve things often make them worse.

Such as, "Let's be reasonable about this. Let's sit down and talk the whole thing out. Surely we can come to some reasonable understanding." Crazy, isn't it? Trying to be reasonable in an unreasonable situation. Even if the issues are based on real problems that could be analyzed, the heat that keeps things going is emotional! And emotions aren't reasonable.

Another common approach is, "Let's put on screws for awhile. A little control will settle this all down." What usually results? — more explosions. In the Chicano/Anglo case mentioned above, father says to son later, "I don't want you seeing that girl again. I don't want my son having anything to do with a girl who flaunts her affection in public. You can't have the car for two weeks." I may not have the language just right, but many of you will recognize the situation. It's the "straw-to-pick-at" sequence.

In many "racial" incidents there is a straw-to-pick-at which prevents progress toward solutions. As long as people keep picking at the one straw, the haystack doesn't budge an inch (centimeter?).

At one time I was part of a group who were trying to help some young people's clubs develop techniques for survival.

Other people were calling them "gangs," "criminal," "racist." But we saw them as the nucleus of community, or cohesiveness, in a place where there was little to hold people together.

Many of these "clubs" would tangle with each other, usually out of an "insult" or competitive dating. In the midst of one of these hassles, some pushing around and actual fights started in a local high school.

The reaction of officialdom was police, and lots of them. The school seemed like a surrounded armed camp. Of course, the situation was escalated, it got worse rather than better.

The police didn't like it. They got more and more uptight as they saw their own failure. We could see them gearing up for an incident they could "make an example of."

Of course, the clubs were also getting more and more uptight, with each other and with the police interference. Frustrated action provoked new threats. Certain words were dropped, just loudly enough, as club members sauntered by police ("pig ... slime ... your mother ...").

Action and reaction, common sense was being used by all parties. Official common sense: "If they are out of control, control them" Club common sense: "If they think they can control us that way, we'll show them." But what was needed was some *un*common sense.

People in our group were known by members of all the clubs. We took a calculated risk and invited all the club leaders to a "War Council" on neutral territory. (Note that we didn't use "common sense" and call for a "Peace Council," involving police, clubs, schools.) The club leaders agreed. When they came together, all weapons were put in a drawer. One of our group acted as chairperson and started out, "O.K., everything's uptight. How would you describe what's happening?" For about three hours everyone dumped accusations and threats on each other. It was pretty grim, but it was necessary for all parties to hear that their opponents had real grievances.

When it got down to "what are we going to do about it?" the clubs had moved a long way by seeing each other as "we." Someone raised the question if the clubs should allow the police to keep them at war with each other.

To make a long story short, they took control of their own destiny, cooled their conflicts, recognized the dignity of differences, thereby taking the power away from the officials and to themselves.

One of the most important principles in settling conflicts is that people do not have to like each other; they just need to find a way to survive together, to get along with each other. So many plans fail because they are aimed at getting people to like each other, rather than putting up with each other.

"Dad, I know it might be hard for you to like my new boy friend, and that's O.K. All I ask is that you try to be nice to him when he comes to visit." That is a lot easier to take than, "I just really dig Jimmy, and I know you are going to like him, too. Oh, you just *have* to like him, Dad." Especially if your dad's a farmer who works to exhaustion daily, and Jimmy is a thin, slight math freak who wears gold-rimmed glasses. Your dad is more likely to tolerate Jimmy, even like him, if he feels he doesn't have to.

"Love they neighbor" might be nice, but is it very realistic? There's no way we can require people to love each other, but we can require that they don't hurt each other, that they put up with each other, in families and communities. I have always liked the way an old teacher of mine put it: "Peace is not the absence of conflict, but the restoration of community."

But what about some practical suggestions? What if you get caught in the middle of what might be called a "racial problem?"

Let's deal with things at the personal/friend/family level first:

1. Realize that even though you might have everything clear in your own head, some of those around you might not. If you start getting funny messages from people because you are keeping company with someone from another racial group, draw them out about it. Don't guess what they are thinking; you could be wrong. Ask in a non-accusatory way, "I have a feeling something's wrong between us. I'd like to know. Would you be willing to talk about it?" Then listen. Don't start defending yourself. Don't assault them with your need to have them share your point of view. Show your maturity by asking to hear their opinion. To listen to it doesn't mean you agree with it.

2. If you think trouble may be developing about a personal relationship, try to make a plan in advance. (See chapters 2 and 3 for help here.) If no trouble develops, you are ahead of the game. If your plan helps to minimize or avoid trouble, you're ahead of the game as

well. It does no good to lament, "Why can't people love and under-stand each other?" If the relationship is important to you, make a plan to preserve it. Again, remember to make a plan for a trial period. If it's not working, go back to the drawing board. Come up with a new plan – don't stick with a loser.

3. If nothing works, change direction. If people won't come around or move an inch toward your point of view, abandon the attempt. Instead, look for a way to divert them, to just get the heat off you so you can do your own thing privately.

Secondly, what about institutional/community level problems?

1. Look for an approach that uses uncommon sense (see above). Rather than aiming straight at the situation, come at it from the side, with a plan where people have things to do. Make plans that get people working *toward* a solution, rather than a plan that is a solution in itself. (This kind usually fails because there are so many people involved who want them to fail.) *Under*state goals, and have clear goals that you can evaluate (see Chapter 3). Not, "We want to improve relations between students of all races in our school," but rather, ask the question, "What would be happening differently in our school if relations between races were beginning to improve?" Then develop goals and plans from answers to that question.

2. Let people of all persuasions be heard. It's not necessary to agree with everything that is heard, but it is necessary that everyone has a chance to be heard. If people are put down for their opinions and ideas, they must hold them even more strongly to maintain their own dignity. It's the old child game, "You did not," "I did so," "You did not," and so on, and so on, and so on.

3. If people are polarized in one of these "and so" games, it is often helpful to stop and start your planning many times. Don't go on endlessly, letting people punish each other with the same arguments, over and over. Find a way to stop and start over again later – "It looks like we're not getting anywhere, let's take a break until three this afternoon and begin again." If people can have some home-work to do meanwhile, like getting information about something, that may help as well.

4. If you are involved in an official way, such as a committee

that is supposed to come up with some solutions, there are some good resources published and organizations that specialize in dealing with these sorts of difficulties (one example, University Associates, La Jolla, California).

What I have suggested here is not a cure-all; there is none. I have outlined some beginning steps that people can take to find a way through problems labelled "racial."

The key is not "Love they neighbor," but rather, "How can I learn to get along with my neighbors, even when I don't like them?"

PART II: VIGNETTES

THE CHILD

I used to be a child
Tumbling through an eternal meadow of innocence.
Like smoke set loose, I drifted endlessly.
Dancing in the breeze
I wandered, feeling the warmth of sun on my face
    or on my back as I knelt to pocket tiny
    magical wonders.
Running — feet pounding against the knotted grasses,
Falling — to lie panting with arms and legs out-
    stretched
I would gulp the warm sweet air and squint into
    the sun.
I remember, just yesterday, I was a child.
And now with each setting sun
I see, in the dusky light, a small meadow
    that is melting slowly before it vanishes.

—Erika Krupp

*   *   *   *   *   *   *

IMOGENE

Sometimes families can mean trouble. Imogene had a stepfather, he was something else. Imogene was seventeen, and she was really sexy. Though her stepfather didn't come right out and say it, he wanted to go to bed with her.

It came out in funny ways. He ordered her around, made her do all kinds of household chores. He yelled and screamed at her if she was even five minutes late coming home, and worst of all, he'd beat her, sometimes start choking her (one of the bruises on her neck wouldn't go away), and once he'd even pulled a knife on her. She was beside herself, not knowing what to do.

Mom wasn't any help. She was on welfare, drank a lot, and didn't want to do anything that would cause her to "lose her man."

Imogene decided to be really brave and went in to see a counselor at the school whom she had heard from the other kids "had some unusual ways of helping people, and he won't fink on you, either."

"I'm really afraid to be here," she said. "If he ever found out I'd come and told anyone about it, he'd kill me for sure. What am I going to do?"

Well, the counselor listened to her, asked her to give him some details about what happened, how it happened (see Chapter 5). He asked if she could tell pretty much when he was working up to one of his blow-ups. Then he said, "This is going to sound a little crazy, but would you be willing to try something crazy just once? Things couldn't be much worse."

"Yes, I'd be willing to try anything, just so long as my stepfather doesn't find out that I've ever been here to talk to you."

"Next time he starts to yell at you or hit you, just let yourself get twice as upset as you usually do, really look scared, frightened, look really hysterical, start breathing hard and heavy, and get really far out. Then say, 'I'm so upset, I'm just going to have to go down to talk to that psychiatrist at the Mental Health Center!' Then take one more big deep breath and faint on the floor. Just lie there, no matter what he does, keep your cool, and don't blow it. Then wait a few days and come tell me what happens."

You might be surprised, but maybe you're swift enough to figure out what happened. He ran out of the room to get her mother. "Come here quick, your daughter's fainted. I can't do anything with her anymore."

And you know? She didn't get threatened anymore after that. Oh, she got yelled at sometimes, but no more hits or threats.

That proud man didn't want any of his family secrets spilled out before some psychiatrist down at the Mental Health Center. No, sir!

* * * * * * *

ARMANDO

He was sixteen, and only 5'5" tall. Alongside everything else he had to face up to every day, that was hard. He'd been beaten up many times. He was always the last chosen for a side when guys were out playing ball on the vacant lot. Girls teased him. He was sick of being small, tired of being picked on.

Standing there on 81st Street, thinking this all over, life didn't seem to hold much hope for him. "What am I going to do? I've got to find some way to make it a little better."

Half in a fog, he turned to walk away and bumped into a man. He heard a low growl. "Oh, I'm sorry, I didn't see you." The man was blind, and the dog who guided him had begun to protect him. I wonder if a dog might be able to help me with my inconvenient size, wondered Armando.

Friends seemed interested as they noticed Armando with his cute little Doberman puppy, all soft and cuddly. Armando seemed to love the dog so much, talking to it, caring for it, taking it with him everywhere he went, till it seemed almost part of him. He read books on how to train dogs. Max, the puppy, soon learned to listen to what Armando told him, and would do almost anything Armando asked.

As Armando and Max walked down the street to the corner, some nine months later, they both stood tall. Armando wasn't afraid of being beat up anymore. He had a new self-respect, things were beginning to fall into line for him. Surprising what a person can learn, simply from bumping into someone.

Ever wonder what you might have learned today, if you'd noticed.

*   *   *   *   *   *   *

THINGS CAN BE CHANGED BEFORE THEY ARE

The history class was such a drag. That man just stood up there lecturing. It was dull. And when he wasn't lecturing he was yelling at someone. I'd been thrown out of class three times already. If that happened again, I'd probably be suspended, and I didn't want that. Bad as school was, it was where the action was, where my friends were.

That counselor who had been giving the rap in psych the other day said, "People who are in relationship with each other regularly are a family (class, club, church, apartment house, etc.) and the way they act with each other is in balance, so that if anyone in the family changes what they're doing (see Chapter 2) the rest of the people involved will have to change." Then he gave us a concrete example: he stopped talking! It was no time at all before members of the class started to fidget, then giggle, lots of different things started happening.

"I wonder," I thought, "is there anything I can do that might affect the drag of a teacher up there, and not get me in trouble? I know, I'll just stare at his left ear and see what happens."

Well, it wasn't even ten minutes and old Mr. Hardnose stopped lecturing and said, "You know, maybe we should stop awhile and discuss what I've been saying." And that's the first time anyone could remember having a discussion in that class.

Might be something you could try in one of your classes – maybe the same thing, or maybe something more creative.

*   *   *   *   *   *   *

THAT OLD TIME RELIGION

John was out doing his paper route. It was a beautiful fall afternoon. He was having fun, feeling good, tossing the papers on the
doorsteps of the houses — everything was going fine. All of a sudden
a gruff voice sounded behind him. "What's that you've got in your
hand, boy?" And John knew he was in for some hassles.

What was in his hand was a "joint," and that simple fact started
a procession of events that you just wouldn't believe — uptightness,
uptightness all over the place. To the "Hall," a call to the parents,
seeing the Probation Officer, Juvenile Court, three days in Juvie before it was over, then home to Mom and Dad. And, of course, that
wasn't the end, it wasn't really over, not in the least.

John has his own P.O. now. He'd come to see John and John
would go to see his P.O. His folks were uptight for in their mind he
was headed down the sure road to heroin, crime, sin (they were *very*
religious), and who knows what else.

"John, from now on I want you home within five minutes after
school's out, and at least until Christmas vacation, you're not to go
out of this house, anywhere, except to church."

Well, that's a tough one to live with. And as the days went on, it
was tougher and tougher. And John knew that there was no way his
parents were going to understand" and take off the heat. He had to
find himself a way through. And just going to church, well . . .

Wednesday night was prayer meeting night, and Dad came home
a little late. Dinner was rushed, Mom was pushing. "We don't have
much time — meeting begins at 7:30." Jane, John's younger sister,
was getting some heat, too. Even though he didn't really dig going, at
least it was a way out of the house — John seemed to be the only
one enjoying the idea of going to church — and then it hit him. "I
wonder if church might be a way for me to find a way out, to be able
to do things on my own again," he said to himself.

"Mom, hurry up, let's go. I really like the new minister, and I
don't want to be late."

And John became one of the most avid churchgoers you could imagine. He started going to everything that was happening at church, to Youth Group, to Choir, to Prayer Meetings, to Evangelism Committee meetings, and it started to get to be a little rough on his parents. Because they had said he couldn't go out alone, they'd had to take him every time, and they really couldn't complain about doing it because, after all, he was "going to church," doing what they wanted him to do.

John even volunteered to be the janitor for the church. He had to be at the church on Saturday afternoons, when no one else was there, to get the place ready for Sunday.

Then, one Sunday evening came the time he had been looking and hoping for. "Mom, it's time for me to go to Youth Group. Would you please take me so I won't be late?"

"John," said faithful Mom, "if you think I'm going to take you to that church another time today, you've got another thought coming. You can just take the bus!"

"But, Mom, I'm not supposed to go out alone."

"Well, I can't be taking care of you your whole life. You just *go!*"

And from that time on, things started loosening up around the house. Sometimes doing something that's hard for you can make things a whole lot easier for you in the long run.

*   *   *   *   *   *   *

CINDY KNEW HOW

A 4-year-old girl was helping clean the garage with her family, and not liking it at all. It was Saturday, and there are much better things to do on a Saturday, as we all know.

Puzzled, but resourceful, she bore up for a long time. Then, by chance, something flew by.

"Daddy, Daddy, what was that?"

"What was what?" said he.

"That pretty thing that flew by!"

"Oh, that! It's a butterfly."

A puzzled look shadowed her knowing face. The door leading away from drudgery had opened a crack. "Daddy, do flutterbies fart?"

Well, old Dad almost choked. Big brother and little sister giggled. Mom was beside herself. They all doubled up with frenzied laughter. The release was so wonderful there was no stopping it.

Small surprise — there was no more garage cleaning that day!

Cindy knew how to get along. Chances are she wouldn't get into much trouble with her parents or life while growing up. Even at four, she could take what was happening, go with it, and turn it into an asset for herself.

* * * * * * *

WHEN A FRIEND NEEDS HELP, WHAT THEN?

Everyone gets to the place, one time or another, when he sees a friend in trouble and wishes he could help. Believe me, that's a touchy situation for a lot of reasons. You don't want to do anything that's going to spoil the friendship or make things worse, and because the person is a friend, it can be pretty scary trying to figure out how to help.

One of the things to steer clear of is offering advice. In most cases, we usually suggest to friends what works for us. The reason it works for us is that it's specific to us. But remember, it may boomerang if the friend tries it.

Then there's a tendency to talk your friends into getting help. This often makes it difficult for the friend to get help — he has to admit to you that he can't handle it, and he might try to tough it out, just to avoid that embarassment with you.

When a person is in trouble, people around him will often try to act as though nothing is wrong. What kind of message do you think that sets up? The friend starts thinking but is unable to talk about it. "I must really be a sicko, the way they're all acting." This can be the kind of force that pushes the person further into trouble.

Well, then, what can a person do? The only thing that I know that might work in this kind of situation is to go to the friend, lay no requirements on him, and ask what's happening. "Gee, John, what's been happening to you? Things seem different." Then let the person respond.

After that you can draw the person out about everything he is willing to talk about. Keep your own opinions out. Just ask questions to clarify what he's saying. Be very hesitant to make suggestions. Help him to come up with his own suggestions. Be a good listener. The most important thing you can do is to assure him that you are concerned and are listening to him. Make sure he clearly understands you're not so sure that you can be of any help, but that you're willing to listen and give support.

*   *   *   *   *   *   *

A HAIRY PROBLEM

A young man was always being hassled by his father about the length of his hair. His father thought he looked terrible, a disgrace to the family, nothing but a hippy. The son tried to help his father understand his view, but there was no way. His father insisted that he cut his hair.

The son thought about running away. It was really an important issue. He talked to his mother to see if she could be of any help, but she thought it should be shorter, too.

"It's really a tough place to be in," said a friend, "but I heard a crazy idea the other day that you might try. A fellow I know set it up with his barber ahead of time, that the barber would cut just a little bit of hair at a time, while the father watched."

Now that didn't sound perfect, but it sounded better than the trap he was in. After all, he kind of liked his father, so why not try it? So the young man went to his father and said, "Dad, I'd like to have my hair cut just the length you'd like me to have it. I want you to be happy about my appearance. Would you be willing to come to the barber along with me, and tell me when the barber has cut it just the right length?"

"Sure," said Dad, and off they went.

The barber cut about half an inch of hair, and the son turned to his father and asked, "Is that short enough, Dad?"

The father said, "No, it should be a little shorter."

Some of the other men waiting their turn laughed a little.

The barber cut another half inch, and the son asked again, "How about now, Dad?"

The father looked around the room first, just to size things up, and said, "That looks just right, Son."

And both of them left the shop happier people.

If they both hadn't won, they both would have lost.

* * * * * * *

WHEN YOUR FRUSTRATION REACHES TEN
(Jeffrey Whitmore)

To survive in a hostile environment you have to develop defenses — protective techniques — or perish. The drawback is, you have to spend so much time fortifying the defenses, refining the techniques, that you don't have much time for more important things, like living, loving, learning, and growing.

An alternative to the defend-or-perish situation is to leave the hostile environment. A young person who runs away from what he or she feels is an impossible home situation is doing just that.

The term "runaway" is one that is frequently used by such a young person's parents and by the authorities whose job it is to hunt the young person down. The term suggests weakness, an inability to deal with reality, and a flight from responsibility.

On the other hand, we don't call people who escape from concentration camps or Vietnamese Prisoner of War camps "runaways." Nor do we accuse them of weakness, inability to deal with reality, or irresponsibility. We might call them "escapees." We certainly recognize them as courageous individuals who, seeing that there is no means of survival within the hostile environment of the concentration camp, at great risk to their lives, escape.

By the same token, the young person who feels his home situation is so hopeless that he or she must leave it can be thought of as an *escapee*. Far from being a cowardly action, such an escape requires real courage. If the escape attempt is unsuccessful, he or she can expect hassles with the police and courts, a worsened situation at home and the prospect that former friends may no longer be permitted by their parents to associate with such a "bad influence."

And if the escape is successful, there are still problems. Many of the young people who made the crusade to the Haight-Ashbury district during the middle and late sixties found that they had merely moved from one sort of hostile environment to another. They met with exploitation by ripoff artists, malnutrition, disease, drug dependency, and, occasionally, death.

Considering the risks involved, what makes a person decide to split?

Imagine that every person has his own tolerance scale that measures frustration from one to ten. When a person decides to split, he's probably reached ten on his personal tolerance scale.

If you're in a situation where thoughts of packing up and getting out are becoming more and more frequent (everybody considers it at one time or another), perhaps you should check your own unique tolerance scale to see where you stand.

One thing about tolerance scales is that they vary so much from person to person. For example, the teacher in the modern suburban high school finds he's edging toward the ten mark when he hears giggling going on while his face is turned to the blackboard. But the teacher in the rat-infested inner-city school doesn't hit ten until his back is up against the blackboard and a knife is pressed to his throat. The fact of the matter is that both teachers are equally frustrated, but their tolerance scales are a lot different.

Or take the president of a company that finds sales were so high this year that he's going to get a $20,000 bonus above and beyond his regular salary. He feels so good that his frustration level drops to three.

Meanwhile, the elderly woman in the run-down tenement finds a five-dollar bill behind her couch that she never knew she'd lost. She feels so good that her frustration level drops to two.

Or there's Ralph, operating at the six level because he can't use his father's Porsche for the country club dance. He's stuck with the Mustang again.

Pete's operating at the five level. He couldn't borrow his brother's ten-speed to go the the Friday night dance at the recreation center. He's stuck with his three-speed again.

The increases and decreases on the tolerance scale are very real to the persons involved. They feel frustration and relief for different reasons, but their feelings are equally genuine.

So back again to the escapees. Is it time for you to split? Have you hit ten on your scale? It might be worth your while to make a list of the things that send you up to the ten mark. If you're aware just what the frustrations are that push you toward the top, you can sometimes avoid them. Or if they're really unavoidable, you might be able to take actions that will make them less unbearable. The frustrations that are the most dangerous are the ones that sneak up and wallop you from behind.

If you can knock a number ten frustration down to about nine and a half, you'll be able to hold on a little bit longer. With practice, patience, and luck, you might be able to send the tenners down below the five mark.

Any way you look at it, you can be the one to decide, with dignity, whether it's time to be an escapee or not. By keeping on top of the situation — staying or splitting — you don't have to be a "runaway."

* * * * * *

GETTING STARTED

That term paper is staring you in the face. You have some ideas, but it is getting closer and closer to the end of the term and nothing is getting down on paper. Every time you begin to work on it there is some good excuse for putting off writing. Mom needs help with the dishes. I promised Dad I'd cut the lawn, and I'd better do that first. Or cleaning rooms, or taking a bath, or talking with a friend on the phone far longer than you really mean to, or deciding you haven't been spending enough time with the rest of the family, or being so tired you really wouldn't be at your best, so it better wait till tomorrow, or . . . you could fill in a lot more excuses.

And it doesn't only apply to writing papers. Getting letters written, applying for a job, starting an exercise program, beginning a diet, riding the bicycle regularly, all these activities fall into the same bag.

What may help you is the fact that dividing huge tasks into small units can sometimes enable you to get on the track and get them done.

'I can't stand the idea of writing this paper, so every single night I'm going to sit down and write for five minutes. I'm going to write down something, whether it's good, bad, or indifferent. At the end of the five minutes I'll decide whether or not I'm going to write any more that night. And, if I don't feel like it, I won't." At the very least, after ten days you've put in about an hour in actual writing.

"I really should be on this diet to lose a few pounds! But it's so terrible to think about, just eggs and grapefruit and junk like that. I know, I'll try it for just one day, then I'll decide if it's worth going any further." Sometimes making a beginning is enough to get to the end.

The point is, that if huge tasks can be divided into small units, the world can open up for someone who is a real "beginner."

*   *   *   *   *   *   *

GETTING USED TO YOUR BODY

"Boy, am I fat. And ugly, too. How could anyone ever like me. My hair is oily and straight. I'm only five feet four. I walk funny, too."

Some people have trouble liking themselves, and maybe they never will. But lot's of people who don't like themselves have learned to accept themselves and by accepting themselves they've been accepted by others. Maybe that's possible for you.

I'll tell you what "Fat and Ugly" up there did, though I don't know whether it would work for you.

He got the idea from a sex book. Every night before he went to bed, in the privacy of the bathroom with the door securely locked so no one would find out, he'd stand before the full-length mirror on the back of the bathroom door and look at himself. He would touch his hair and say, "That's my hair, I'm not going to have any other, so I accept it." Then on to another part of his body. "That's my chest, I'm not going to have another, I accept." And so on, till he had touched his whole body.

And one day he found himself saying, "You know, that's not so bad a chin you have there, Fred," and it surprised him. And slowly things began to change; he began to accept himself.

Now maybe Fred will never like himself, but he's learned to accept himself, and even to like *some* parts of himself. And others are accepting him as well.

You don't really have to *like* your body to live and have fun; you just need to *accept* it.

Funny how you can love what you accept without even liking it — sometimes!

*   *   *   *   *   *   *

SHY?

It's a long road out from under shyness. And before you start that journey out, how about testing a little bit whether or not you want to change? (Some people really love "shy" people.)

1. What would it be like not to blush when someone tells you you are attractive? Can you think about that?

2. Watch some people who are really bold, who just speak their minds. Maybe you could be on the lookout for them in restaurants, stores, or other public places. Can you see yourself. enjoying being like that? Be honest.

3. Go in your room, get in front of the mirror. Start looking at yourself, very carefully, up and down and all around. Start taking off your clothes, a little bit at a time, watching all the while. Keep going until you are totally unclothed. How do you feel? Are you shy? Are you feeling embarassed or uncomfortable?

4. Try just twice (even though it will be very scary and difficult) to go some place with someone and "act as if" you are not shy for the entire evening (even though you know way down deep inisde that you are still shy).

Once you have completed all these tests, and the results *are* different for everyone — for each person is a unique individual — you'll know, without anyone else in the world telling you, just what YOU want to do.

* * * * * * *

TWO POINTS OF VIEW
(Jeffrey Whitmore)

Angie rushed from the classroom, sobbing with anguish. She had received a "C" on her social studies exam.

Linda rushed from the classroom, sobbing with joy. She had

received a "C" on her social studies exam.

    MORAL: If you always get "A's", then a "C" is a bitch.

                If you think you're going to flunk, though,

                It makes a pleasant switch!

* * * * * * *

YOU'RE ALL WET

I knew an elderly woman who was loved by almost everyone who knew her. Although she was warm and friendly, she had a shyness about her that made her seem more vulnerable than she really was. She seemed to be the perfect sucker for anyone who wanted to take advantage of her.

But she wasn't.

I once asked her how she managed to deal with such people so effectively, since she seemed so shy.

"Well," she said, "I am a bit shy, but I don't let that bother me. Whenever I have to deal with people who try to impress me with their superiority — whether they're vacuum cleaner salesmen or bank presidents — I imagine that they've just wet their pants are are acting high and mighty so I won't find out about it. That takes them down a peg — at least as far as I'm concerned.

* * * * * * *

UNDERSTANDING

If you want to be understood by your parents, that's
    a problem?
If parents try to understand you, they will usually
    misunderstand and aggravate things.
You don't have to understand your parents, they don't
    have to understand you.

Just find a way to get along with each other, live
   with each other!
Celebrate your differences rather than trying to make them go away.
You have your life, they have theirs.

*   *   *   *   *   *   *

PARENTS AND RESTAURANTS

"John, I'm sure you'll want the super hamburger with french fries
and a glass of milk."

Do your parents start making strange noises like that when you
sit down in a restaurant together? Trying to decide for you in backhanded ways what you should eat, because the super hamburger costs
$2.29 and you might choose the fried chicken which costs $3.49.
Would you rather have a clear choice?

Well, it doesn't work for everyone, but it works often enough so
it's worth trying. As soon as you get into the restaurant, beat your
parents to the gun, but do it in a very polite way so that it doesn't
backfire. "Dad, I know you're concerned because restaurants are getting pretty expensive these days, so would you please tell me the
things that you would like me to choose from on the menu? I don't
want to get you upset by choosing something too expensive."

It's very difficult for him to zero in on any *one* thing in response
to a mature question such as the one stated above. He'll probably
point to a number of things and that will give you a lot more choice.
Or he might even say, "Well, for today, why don't we splurge. Pick
anything you'd like."

*   *   *   *   *   *   *

LEAVING HOME

We lived in a poor neighborhood in Boston. We had a large family, and I was the youngest of the lot. I watched as each of my older brothers and sisters moved out on their own, and I yearned to do the same. Mom had been really good to us. I never knew who Dad was.

Finally I was all alone with Mom. She had been good to me, but every time I started to make noises like I was moving on, she'd get sick. I'd settle in and take care of her. Her recoveries would be nothing short of miraculous.

Finally, I'd had it. "Mom, sick or not sick, I've got to move on. I've got a lot of business to take care of."

"Henry," she said, "if you move out, I'll be dead within a week!"

Now talk about fear of the Lord being struck into a boy's heart. I knew she didn't have any money for the funeral. That troubled me. But I knew I had to go — I'd be hopelessly stuck there and so would my Mom if I didn't. I really did care for good old Mom.

So I started telephoning. I called my grandmother, all my brothers, my sisters, and asked them, "Do you have enough money so that you could help pay for Mom's funeral when I move out? She says she'll die in a week if I go."

"No, I'm sorry, I don't" they said, one and all.

I was in a deep quandary. I went to Mom and told my story. "Mom, I've called Grandma and all my brothers and sisters and asked them if they had enough money to help pay for your funeral when I move out, and none of them said yes. So I'll tell you what I'm going to do. I'm going right out and get a job, and I'll save up enough money, real fast, so your funeral will be taken care of just beautifully, and then I'll move out."

Well, you can imagine the storm. She called me every name that I'd ever heard and then some, and threw my butt out of the house right then. "Don't you ever come back!" she said.

That was over ten years ago. Mother's fine and I'm fine. And after about two months of fussing and fuming, and having nothing to do with me, Mom called and said, "I'd like to see you, Son. Would you come by to *visit* some day?"

Now I wonder if you've ever been in a situation where no matter what you did it was wrong, so you did what was a little scary and it turned out OK? Ever happen to you?

*   *   *   *   *   *   *

ANOTHER FIVE-STEP SOLUTION

A girl once wanted a stereo set very much. She didn't have the money for it, and her parents told her that they couldn't afford to buy her one.

Although she sometimes cared for children and did other odd jobs, it seemed as though it would take forever to get enough money for the set.

One day she saw that there was a stereo sale going on at a local discount store. She knew that then was the time to buy, but she just didn't have the cash. She thought about the problem for awhile and finally came up with a possible solution. She knew that her father liked contracts and liked to see her demonstrate her increasing sense of responsibility. "I'll make him an offer he can't refuse," she decided, and she wrote a formal proposal in a letter to him. He liked her idea. They discussed it and came up with an agreement.

Her letter and the resulting contract follow:

Dear Dad:

This letter is in regards to the purchase of my stereo. Since what I have in mind may be quite lengthy, I decided to write, thus saving one big phone bill.

Now, I've given it a lot of thought and I really think that I want the $299 model we saw at Big Western Stereo. If I invest in a poor or used one, it may not work very well or very long. Whereas a good one, even though it may be more expensive to me at the time of purchase, would prove to be a good investment to me as: (a) if I ever wanted to add to my system, it would be worthwhile; (b) I can use it when I move away from home, i.e., when (if) I go away to college. At any angle, I think it is wiser of me to do this (or at least try).

The other matter is that of my financial status. I figure that since you said you would contribute $60 to my cause I will have to pay approximately $240. There is a problem, though. The sale price on this stereo system will most likely last only a short while, giving me only a short time to act. And since there is no chance of my saving enough money right now, I propose this: that you pay the total amount of the stereo and I will pay *you* by means of one $35 payment every 1½ months. This will take about twelve months. How does this sound to you?

I know that you people are a bit low on money now, but this is the only way I would ever be able to afford a really good stereo. I will, though, save every cent I get in order to possibly pay you before payments are due. I know that this is a very serious thing on my part and that I have to be very responsible about it.

As this would be the biggest transaction I've made in my life, I also hope to learn to manage things better from it.

Well, then, all I can say is please give this some serious thought, and if you have any other alternatives in mind, please call me. I'm willing to try anything within reason.

Love you,
Jane

CONTRACT BETWEEN JANE DOE AND JOHN DOE

Dated: February 1972

TERMS OF THIS AGREEMENT:

1. John Doe will buy stereo set described in special sale advertisement, in order to take advantage of the sale. This stereo will remain his property until the terms of this contract have been met in full. It shall remain in the custody and under the care of Jane, however, contingent upon the terms of this agreement, especially as outlined in Article 5.

2. Total cost of the stereo is (including tax) $309.95
   Down payment, representing parents' birthday
   and Christmas presents to Jane   60.00
                                       Balance $249.94

This amount was charged on Master Charge, to be paid by Jane, including interest.

3. Jane's payments shall be as follows:

April 1	$35.00
June 15	35.00
August 1	35.00
September 15	35.00
November 1	35.00
January 15	35.00
March 1	35.00
April 15	35.00
Interest	50.00
Final Payment on June 1	$19.49

4. If all the payments are made on time, John agrees to pay the interest, thus making final payment of $4.94 on April 15.

5. If Jane does not make payments on time, and a payment should become due 30 days late, on the 31st day after payment is due she will return custody of the stereo to John until the payment is made.

6. It is also agreed that Jane may make payments in smaller amounts, at varying times, as she sees fit, as long as the total amount of the payments does not fall behind the schedule which is outlined above.

THIS AGREEMENT IS SIGNED THIS 18th day of February, 1972.

Signed: _____
                (Jane Doe)
_____

(A record of payment chart follows on the actual contract.)

*   *   *   *   *   *   *

IT'S ALL RELATIVE
(Jeffrey Whitmore)

When speaking with officers, enlisted men in the army are required to call them "Sir." For most enlisted men, the "Sir" business becomes a habit, and they never think twice about it.

Not so with Specialist Four Von Tress, a legal clerk.

"I have to say 'Sir' to second lieutenants who are younger than I am," he complained to his barracks mates, "and I don't even call my grandfather, 'Sir.'"

His fellow enlisted men were not impressed.

"That's your grandfather's problem."

"That's the army way."

"That's life."

But Von Tress was not satisfied. Through the night he brooded, concentrating his dark genius on the vexing problem. What choices did he have? He could say "Sir" to all the officers and suffer inner anguish. He could *not* say "Sir" to them and suffer the conseuqences of insubordination. He could avoid talking with them altogether, but that would be difficult since he worked in a headquarters filled with officers.

Finally, with the dawn, he was enlightened. Just as it had come to Einstein many years before, the thought came to him: "It's all relative."

When it came time to report for duty, Sp4 Von Tress entered his office and greeted the second lieutenant who was in charge of the legal section. "Good morning, Sir" he said heartily.

"Good morning, Von Tress," the pink-cheeked lieutenant replied.

"Good morning, Sir," Von Tress said to the private first class whose desk was next to his.

"Good morning, Sir," he said to his desk.

"Good morning, Sir," he said to his typewriter.

"Good morning, Sir," he said to his chair.

And so it went from then on with Sp4 Von Tress, he "Sirred" his officers, he "Sirred" his friends, he "Sirred" the inanimate objects that surrounded him. There was no way he could be considered insubordinate, for he never forgot to say "Sir."

When he was discharged from the army, it was with no little pleasure that he visited his grandfather and called him "Sir." And his grandmother as well.

* * * * * * *

A FIVE-STEP PROBLEM-SOLVING PARABLE

Once upon a time there was a young man (just 12 years old) who said that he had a problem: his parents never talked to him. Now that he had (1) defined his problem, he (2) looked around his house to figure out what he could do about it. Things seemed pretty normal, just like many other American homes. Life pretty much revolved around a big color TV set, but he wasn't very interested in it. He was interested in active sports and music. He (3) tried very hard to talk to them, but to no avail. He asked his grandmother to talk to them, which only made them angry. He tried to get them to look at his homework. He then (4) became upset because he wanted his parents to share in his activities.

But his parents were interested, as mentioned, in TV. In fact, when they came home from work (they both worked outside of the home), Mom would rush to make dinner while Dad was taking his shower. The TV was already on, and Mom was watching it through the archway into the living room as she cooked. The young man would try to help with dinner and try to talk to his mother.

But when Dad got out of the shower, they all sat down to eat in front of the big color TV. "Shush," said Dad, "I'll miss what Ed Cronkite is saying."

"Shush," said Mom, "I'll miss the weather."

And so it went, night after night after night.

Well, the young man thought and thought and thought. "What

can I do to change this situation and get to talk with my folks?" Then he came up with a plan. "If I try," he said to himself, "in a different way to tell them it's all right if they watch TV, maybe they'll talk to me."

So very shyly, he (5) went to his Dad and said, "You know, Dad, sometimes I'm really thankful that you and Mom watch TV as much as you do. And I don't want to make you angry when I say this, but because you watch TV so much, I get away with a lot of stuff around here that the other kids I know can't get away with."

And the young man and his mother and father have been talking ever since.

*   *   *   *   *   *   *

LONGING FOR A LOST LOVER

It really hurts when you've loved someone deeply, and with little or no warning and no explanation they up and leave. "It's over between us, Jim. I guess I'm just a free spirit and can't stay related to just one guy."

That's a hard, hard place to be in — there's nothing you've really done to lose her, you're totally left out of the decision, and it hurts. There's really no other way to put it. It hurts like hell!

People in this kind of situation will do many things: some talk of suicide; others of running away (afraid to let friends know that IT has happened); others hole up, stay away from people and cry a lot; others get angry, lash out, and try to let everyone know how bad their former partner has been. Just about anything that people can dream up can happen when a close relationship ends — especially when it is a one-sided choice.

Now what needs to happen for you to get over the lost lover is very simple but very difficult: you have to get past the old relationship and into new ones. In a very real sense, the person in the old relationship has to be "dead." Dead in the sense that you get past the hope that he or she will return and everything will be happiness and peace and love from that point on.

There's only one way that I know to do that, and it can be very painful, very difficult. It's to find a person — could be a friend, could be a parent (though it's very unusual to have this kind of relationship possible with a parent), could be a teacher or counselor, minister, priest, or relative — no matter who it is, it has to be someone who you are confident is really willing to share the depth of your emotion, to allow you to express whatever feelings you want to express.

And what's the process? Set aside a good bit of time — two or three hours the first time — and start telling that helping person, whom you yourself have chosen, all the things that happened on that day when you found out, right up to the moment you found out, in as much detail as you can remember. And what happened just after you found out.

Then go back and tell what happened the day before you found out, again right up on and through the time when you found out, in all the infinite things that you can remember, both good and bad.

Keep doing this, letting *your* helping person put in his or her comments (which you don't have to agree with, by the way), going back a day further in time every time you do it, for as much time as you have to spend.

If you don't feel relieved after the first time that you've done this, set up another time. In one of the sessions, sooner than you think (and you will know it by yourself), you will make the leap into the present, and everything will be OK. The grief will be over, and you can begin again with the life that seemed over. It might take you one session or five, three or eight, two or fourteen. No matter how many it takes, you'll know when it happens and you'll feel free.

*   *   *   *   *   *   *

CHANGING HABITS

Sometimes in your life you can come up against something that's not really a problem but just something that you'd like to change. It's usually a habit that you've been stuck with for a long time, like biting your nails; being sarcastic with people (without knowing it); frowning all the time; losing your temper; getting tongue tied; just lots of things.

One plan that's often effective with this kind of difficulty is to choose a friend who spends a lot of time with you and who would be willing to help you and set up with him a "signal for change."

It goes like this. Let's say you are often sarcastic with people when you don't want or mean to be. It turns them off, and makes it difficult for you to establish new friendships. You might even be losing some old ones, too, because of it. Maybe it happens with teachers and parents. You just drive them up the wall, make them angry, and break down communication.

So get together with the friend who's willing to help. Explain the situation fully and then ask, "When you're with me, would you be willing to give me a signal every time I start being sarcastic in the way that we have just discussed?" If your friend agrees, all that's left is to figure out what an appropriate signal might be.

Maybe your friend could reach over and touch you on the back of the hand, every time it happens. Maybe a strategic cough, one that's unique, which you both understand (this one can be used in a classroom, even when your friend's on the other side of the room). Maybe he will tug at his nose or ear. There are an infinite variety of types of signals that you can figure out just for you.

And what should happen when you get the signal from your friend? It shouldn't mean "stop," but only to "pause" for just a few seconds. You could count to ten in your mind when you get the signal. Then decide, "Do I want to keep doing what I'm doing or not?" There might be certain times when you want to be sarcastic!

Use your imagination. This is a tool that can be used to change lots of things that you yourself would like to change. And *no* one has to know a thing about what's going on except you and your signaling friend.

*   *   *   *   *   *   *

BREAKING UP

There are so many ways that couples break up and so many reasons for break ups, that it's difficult to generalize about the subject. One fact I do know: it's usually very hard for at least one-half of the couple. There can be tears, anger, fights, sleeplessness, hours and hours of talking, feelings of being cheated — almost anything's possible.

A friend told me that when he was a teen-ager, just before every summer, most of the guys would break up with their "steadies," because they lived near a resort and they knew there would be all sorts of new girls around for the summer.

On one occasion, in middle June, he was sitting with his "steady" (an ancient term to be sure) in a movie. It was a Doris Day movie. He was going to tell his girl that he was breaking up with her sometime during the movie. He decided, "I'll count to one hundred in my mind, and when I reach one hundred I'll open my eyes and tell her." Which he did, and as he turned back to the screen to focus on the movie again to avoid the gaze of his girl frield, Doris Day started singing, "Love me or leave me, and let me be lonely." What timing! His girl stood up, threw his ring at him, and went sobbing out of the theater.

Now this one worked out OK because of Doris Day. Because of the timing of that song on the screen, the girl felt free to scream and express her deep hurt.

But under normal circumstances, in this setting, the girl would have had to be quiet, not make any fuss, and that, of course, was the reason my friend had chosen that location.

The point of all this is, if you're going to break up, do it in a private place where both of the people involved can have the right to their sorrow and strong feelings. It's a lot harder to do this at first, but it makes it a lot easier to get over the sorrow and the bad feelings in the end. And it takes a lot less time.

If a girl breaks up with a guy by never telling him, just ignoring him, it can take months for him to get over the hurt. If she faces him head on, tells it like it is, even though it hurts a lot at first, there's dignity to it, and he can get over that a lot more quickly.

All it really amounts to is giving a person that's meant a lot to you just a little decent respect when it comes time to change the relationship.

* * * * * * *

LEARNING TO OBSERVE

One of the ways to avoid hassles is to have the ability to know what's going on. People get into situations where they feel sure they're right about something and suddenly the situation falls apart and the response follows, "Well, I didn't know that was going to happen."

For example, you can think your mother is really becoming a bitch, just totally unreasonable. You get into huge hassles with her and the two of you get totally polarized. Maybe, just maybe, if you had learned to be a good observer, you would have noticed that she'd been going to the doctor a little more frequently, that she almost always seemed to be having a period, that she was complaining about headaches, and so on — and you've guessed it already — your so-called "bitchy" mother is merely suffering some of the problems of change-of-life (menopause).

I'd like to suggest that you start learning to be a better observer; that you learn to look beyond the surface of what's happening and try to see what's happening at many levels. The following suggestions will help you become a better observer.

1. Go into the middle of a large supermarket. Close your eyes, stand there for 10 minutes or so. What do you hear, smell? How are

you treated?

2. Put on some really grubbyclothes and go into the fanciest store in town. Pay attention to how you are treated, to what people do. If anyone says anything to you, don't panic, say, "I'm just looking." How do you feel?

3. Go to the airport. Let yourself get the feel of the place. Look around, see what you can see. Look at the people, what are they doing? What is the main mood? How does the place sound? Do you want to go somewhere? Pay attention to a single family. What can you tell by the way they are acting?

4. Spend four hours *alone* in a location such as a beach, forest, field, park, shopping center, subway, etc. What happens? How do you feel? What sights, sounds, smells do you record?

5. Go to a church that you don't usually attend. Pay attention to how people treat you. What's going on?

6. Pay very close attention to what your mother and father, brothers and sisters do for an entire evening. What can you learn from the observation?

* * * * * * *

THINGS YOU HAVE A RIGHT TO KNOW

Did you know

. . . that no other person can know what feels good to you without your telling them?

. . . that masturbation does not cause pimples, insanity, or make you anti-social?

. . . that what your friends or other people choose to do for themselves sexually is OK, whether you choose to do it for yourself or not?

. . . that what you choose to do for yourself is OK whether your friends choose to do it or not?

. . . that there is a lot of information about human sexuality available in books?

. . . that there is no physical danger in becoming sexually aroused and not having an orgasm — either for males or for females? And if it's uncomfortable, it's always possible to masturbate.

. . . that you have a right to decide for yourself whether you want to date one person or several people at one time?

. . . that you won't be liked any better if you say yes when you really want to say no?

. . . that your mother and father probably had many of the same feelings and concerns when they were your age as you have?

. . . that sexual activity doesn't make you hip? You're hip when you make choices that feel good to you at the time and which don't intentionally hurt another person.

*   *   *   *   *   *   *   *

IF YOU LOVE MORE THAN ONE

If you compare, beware
    but celebrate the differences
    love the differences
    carry no secrets
    while not talking about others
    and you might
       have a chance
    to love more than one.

*   *   *   *   *   *   *

HERE COMES ANOTHER ONE,
WORSE THAN THE OTHER ONE

Boyfriends can be a problem in lots of ways, and one of the ways that's tough to deal with comes up when your parents don't like him. They might think he's too rough or tough, that he dresses wrong, has the wrong family, smells bad, or just lots of things.

When this situation happens the *more* you try to talk Mom and Dad into accepting the boyfriend, the *less* they are willing to accept him. And probably the *more* you'll like him. A terribly frustrating place to be.

So you probably don't want to get them to like him; that would take away some of the excitement around him. But you'd like them to accept him a little bit, so they'll let you go out with him.

A girl I know tried a very creative thing. When her parents expressed displeasure at a boyfriend — who was really a nice guy, not someone they really had to worry about — she made a little plan. She asked a boy, one she knew was far less acceptable to her parents than her real boyfriend, if he would be willing to come home with her and pretend that he was her boyfriend when she introduced him to her parents.

He did and the parents were horrified, of course. Things got worse, and soon they asked what had happened to John. "He seemed like such a nice sort of guy," they said.

Sometimes to do what you want, you have to find a way to do what you don't want for a short time.

*   *   *   *   *   *   *

FRIENDS AND GIRLS AND GUYS
AND BEING CLOSE AND RELATIONSHIPS

"*I* don't want to get caught up in all this courting nonsense, it's all such a game. *Why* are *we* always testing each other? *Why* won't *you* be honest with me?

Some key words are *italicized* above. They appear in both open relationships and in those that aren't so open. But if you'd like to be close without being stifled, to avoid a lot of the boy/girl nonsense, knowing a little bit about these key words can help.

Why almost always means "justify yourself." It's hard to be close and open if you're always being asked to justify yourself. No one ever says, "Why are you on time tonight?" It's always, "Why are you late again?"

If there are a lot of "why's" in your talk, it will be tough to be close. Along with most "why" sentences is the implication that something is wrong with the way the other has acted: "Why didn't you call me last night?" Often this has the implication of "probably because you were out with someone else."

You, we, and *they* sentences are also ways of accusing. "You *should* have opened the door for me," is an accusation. And "should" is one of those trap words, too — "should" implies that the other person *ought* (and that's another of those trap words) to be able to read your mind.

The key to being close, to avoiding stifling relationships, is to represent *yourself*, not the other person, and to be honest when you do. That's where the *I*, that *I* italicized, comes in. If you begin your sentences with "I" when it comes to representing yourself in your personal relationships, it's very difficult to accuse — to ask someone to justify himself. It also makes it possible for him or her to respond to you, not to be a smokescreen that only a mind reader could see through.

"I was upset when I saw you out with Terry," is very different than saying, "*Why* did *you* go out with Terry. *You ought* to apologize for that."

"I think *you should*," is not an "I" message. It's a backhanded way of making a *you* statement. Represent yourself, tell how you feel, and *you* will know more of the joy of close and unstifled relationships. "I liked writing this! I hope you enjoy reading it."

* * * * * * *

CONTRACTS, AGREEMENTS, GETTING ALONG

When people begin to live together, whether they are friends sharing an apartment or people getting married, many ordinary daily problems can be avoided if people think through what they want their relationship to be, and make an agreement.

Agreements have to be tailored precisely to the needs of the people involved in order for them to work. One that is a good agreement for me might be a very bad agreement for you. Many so-called "communes" have disintegrated with the loving people in them coming to the point of hating each other because of a lack of clear understanding of how (an agreement) they would live their lives together. Many marriages of long standing come apart at the seams because one partner changes the rules in mid-marriage, and there is no vehicle for dealing with such a change in rules.

In most relationships it is not the big issues that split people, but the little nit-picking things that accumulate because they're "not big enough to make an issue of." Someone is getting put down all the time. One person gets all the dirty work. One person never picks up after himself. Someone leaves a mess in the bathroom all the time. Another is always late.

What follow are two examples of agreements. The first is a contract that a couple I know made in conjunction with their marriage. The second is an example of an agreement which two women made before they began sharing an apartment with each other. These examples are not meant to be "shoulds," that which you *should* do, but are meant to be illustrations which will prod your imagination to come up with agreements, when it is appropriate in your life, that are exactly fitted to your individual needs. Taking time to make such agreements can save a person an awful lot of grief!

MATRIMONIAL AGREEMENT (MARRIAGE SETTLEMENT)

This agreement is entered into June 1, 1984, between Helen Heat and Bob Strong.

PREAMBLE: This document expresses the wishes and represents principles designed to supplement our marital vows and obligations entered into by virtue of the marriage ceremony we participated in on June 1, 1984. It is our general purpose and mature recognition that matrimony should not automatically stifle and restrict the spiritual freedoms and legal rights associated with single persons. Rather, matrimony should secure these individual values and provide a foundation for new values to be shared and secured by our marriage.

To fulfill this purpose we endorse and agree to abide by the ensuing Principles:

(1) Helen and Bob may each choose to use their own surname or the other's surname.

(2) No children shall result from our marriage, either by birth or adoption, unless there is a separate agreement authorizing children. Such agreement shall make provision for child custody, visitation, and child support, in case of termination of the marriage. Furthermore, there shall be no children during the initial two years of marriage. In the event there are: (a) children born or adopted without an agreement providing for the matters discussed above, and (b) a termination of the marriage as discussed in paragraph 4, then the questions of custody, visitation, and child support shall be determined by the arbitrators provided for in paragraph 5, on the basis of what is best for the child or children.

(3) Annually, before May 15, we agree to examine and evaluate our marriage for purposes of clarifying and communicating about the nature of our relationships as individual persons and as married people; and to set in writing our contractual relationship which shall

follow the present contract.

(4) We agree to remain married for a minimum of two years. In the event that we desire to terminate our marital relationship, we will do so entirely through our own personal capacities.

(5) In the event of such a termination, distribution of property acquired during our marriage shall be determined by a three-person arbitration team, one appointed by each of us, and the third chosen mutually by the two who were appointed individually.

(6) Further, in the event of such a termination, we agree there shall be no alimony payable by Bob or Helen to the other.

(7) Our purpose is to share the responsibilities of our household, working this out as we go, formally and informally.

(8) Whereas, in the period of our marriage we will make significant joint financial commitments, and whereas we may come up against issues where we cannot agree, and wereas we wish to provide for those economic and occupational alternatives which fulfill the purposes stated in the Preamble, we agree that:

(a) Neither of us will incur a financial obligation exceeding $100 without the agreement of the other;

(b) At the request of either party, such mutual financial decisions, or decisions with respect to other issues where there is not clear agreement, shall follow research and careful consideration in two formal meetings, one to assign information gathering tasks to each other, the second to review the information and make a decision;

(c) If we cannot agree on such a major decision, we shall institute an arbitration team as described in paragraph 5.

(9) Any further agreements necessary to implement and authenticate the general and specific principles set forth in this document shall be prepared and executed by us.

(10) The provisions of this agreement shall be separate and apart from each other, and if any part of it shall be determined to be unenforceable or void as far as the courts are concerned, the remaining portions shall remain in force and be enforceable as far as the law and the courts shall provide at the particular time.

(11) This document is to be considered an addendum to Marriage Certificate No. 11111, filed in Sam Hill, California, Tudor County,

pertaining to the marriage consummated on June 1, 1984 between us.

The period of the present contract is from the date of signing to June 1, 1985.

Witnesses: Signatures:

_____   _____

_____   _____

* * * * * * *

AGREEMENT TO LIVE TOGETHER

We are going to share an apartment. We want to have a good time together and avoid hassles so in this contract we will try to plan for the business of our household.

Paying the Bills

Gail has a knack for this, so she will be responsible for paying the rent, the telephone, utilities, and any other bills we decide to split 50-50. We will both keep track of any long distance and message-unit phone calls on a pad by the telephone.

Elizabeth will pay her share of standard monthly expenses on the first of the month. Gail will pay all bills during the first week in the month and then tell Elizabeth if any extra is needed. Gail will keep a special notebook of our finances, partly so that they don't get mixed up and partly so that Elizabeth can take over the job more easily if Gail gets tired of it.

If either of us decides to move out, she will give one month's notice (at least) and help the other find a new roommate.

Buying and Preparing Food

We will try a combination of doing some of this independently and some together. Generally, we will keep a "cash kitty" for buying things on our list of staples and cleaning supplies and food we share at dinners. At first we will each put in $15 a week and see how that works.

We will take turns, for a week at a time, being in charge of the kitchen. That will mean buying these foods and supplies, cooking dinners, washing dishes, taking out garbage, and keeping the kitchen clean. Every Sunday night, when we do our regular planning, we'll mark on a calendar the nights when we'll eat together.

Each of us will be in charge of our own breakfast and lunch. We will also clean up after ourselves. We'll each have a special place in the refrigerator and in the cupboards to store foods that we buy just for ourselves. That way we'll know that food in other places may be shared, no matter who has bought it.

Keeping House

Our bedrooms are private. We can keep them as neat or messy as we like.

The bathroom might be the hardest place to share, so we will be extra careful about keeping our things neat and not monopolizing the room at busy times. It will help that we go to work at different times.

We've already discussed the kitchen.

As for the living room, we will try to keep it neat, not leave things lying around, etc.

Once a week we will clean house together. Since a lot of weekends will be booked up, we'll choose a mutual time for cleaning each week when we do our planning on Sunday night. We will each do our own laundry, since most of our clothes, sheets, and towels will be our own things.

Privacy

At the same time that we are excited about living together, we know we could blow the whole thing if we abuse each other's need for privacy.

Of course, our bedrooms are private. Our clothes and personal possessions are private, too. Generally, we'll enjoy sharing things, but we will always ask. We will never go looking through the other person's things or "borrowing" without asking.

We will try to respect the privacy of feelings, too. If one of us is feeling down or upset, the other will try to be sensitive and not bug her. However, probably the best way for this to work is for the moody-one-of-the-moment to say so ("I'm feeling rotten, and I'd rather not talk about it").

As far as other things, like one of us playing loud music while the other needs to study, or like having guests, we'll just try to use common courtesy and keep open communications. Whenever possible, we'll clear it ahead of time when we're going to bring guests in. If this kind of thing happens spontaneously, we'll just be prepared to be respectful of the other person, and go into the bedroom, if necessary, to avoid disturbing her.

Weekly Planning

We'll have a special time weekly — Sunday, 9 p.m. — to do any planning we need to do (like dinner schedules). At that time we'll also try to bring up anything that may have been bugging us, but that there didn't seem to be the right time for before. Usually, these meetings will be short, but we plan to do them faithfully anyway, to keep communications open and to prevent problems from developing.

Time of This Contract

This contract will be for 3 months, beginning when we move in together. At the end of 3 months, we will discuss the whole thing again. Maybe we'll renew it. Maybe we'll change a little or a lot. If we make a new contract, we will take the time to type it up and sign it because then we think we'll take it more seriously.

Date: _____

Witnesses: Signed: _____

_____   _____

_____

*   *   *   *   *   *   *

BAD DAYS MAKE GOOD MEMORIES

A young person came to a wise old man and asked what he could tell him by the way of help and guidance in life. The old man said, "Success in my life endeavor depends upon good judgment."

The young person said, "Thank you, but how do I get good judgment?"

The old man replied, "Good judgment comes from experience."

"Thank you again, very much, but how do I get experience?"

"Oh, that's simple — experience comes from bad judgment."

* * * * * * *

PRIVATE PARTS

A girl I know was out on a date with a guy for the first time. It had been a good evening. She did like him, but wasn't totally convinced he was her kind of guy.

As they arrived in front of her house, he turned off the motor and began to draw her close to him. His words were of her beauty, her personality, the way she turned him on. He began to rub his nose gently in her hair, commenting how sensuous the aroma and texture of it was. As he kissed her gently on the cheek, his left hand began its assent up her left thigh, his right hand holding firmly to her shoulder, drawing her closer yet.

"Hey, wait a cotton pickin' minute! What in the world do you think you are doing? Do you see this handbag of mine? Would you go feeling around in there without asking?"

"No, of course, not, that's your private purse."

"Well, where your hand is going, that's private too, and I'm not so sure I want you feeling around there either."

Sometimes private parts are as private as purses.

* * * * * * *

MASTURBATION – TOUCHING TO ORGASM

Most people have masturbated, either knowingly or unknowingly. Even the word is "dirty" to lots of people. If fact, some parents are more uptight over whether or not their children masturbate than whether or not they do well in school.

One thing for sure, there are many strange notions about masturbation. For about forty years most mental illnesses were blamed on masturbation. They were lumped into the category, "masturbatory insanity" – a totally unfounded idea perpetrated on the world by some doctors who didn't know what they were talking about, and who were sexually hung up themselves.

There are a lot of interesting myths associated with masturbation – those who masturbate grow hair on the palms of their hands; they get pimples; turn into homosexuals; their penis or clitoris will wither and drop off; masturbation will take away womanliness or manliness; it will make your penis bend so it will be hard to get in when you start having intercourse with women; mature women only experience orgasm through penis in vagina; and many, many more!

All of these things are pure myth! Not a one is founded in fact, and there are hundreds of other ideas associated with masturbation that are also untrue.

There is almost no way you can hurt yourself (a favorite phrase of parents telling their children why they shouldn't masturbate) masturbating – and let's get away from that word. Its literal meaning is to "putrify yourself." Touching yourself to orgasm, or stimulating yourself to orgasm can't really hurt you. Even if you get into doing it almost continuously, compulsively, you would either give up out of boredom, or because you were too sore to continue before you could do yourself any physical harm.

Of course, there can be emotional harm – but because of the trips that others lay on you, or you lay on yourself, not from anything related to self-stimulation.

Many parents lay a guilt trip on children – so, guys will masturbate with a sock over their penis, so spots won't get on the sheets; or learn to come (ejaculate) in 44.3 seconds so they won't get caught, thereby teaching themselves to be premature ejaculators, making lots of problems for themselves when later they begin to get it on with women. There just aren't that many women around who come to orgasm 44.3 seconds after insertion. or gals, only touching themselves while in the bath because they have been given the message, "It's dirty down there, shouldn't touch." At least guys are told they are being "good," even by uptight parents, when they aim straight, don't dribble on the floor, etc.

So, to make things clear — research shows (Masters and Johnson and others) people who learn to stimulate themselves to orgasm without guilt, truly loving themselves, seem to have far better and more trouble free relationships, sexually and otherwise.

Men, take your time. Teach yourself to take at least fifteen minutes stimulating yourself before orgasm — who wants to be a premature ejaculator. Lay back and enjoy it, let your imagination go, learn to savor that time with yourself — real "self respect."

Women, do the same. Learn what feels good to you in the way of stimulation so you can share it with your partner when the time is right. Learn what orgasm is all about. Learn that most women can come to orgasm in less than five minutes through self-stimulation. Let your fantasies go where they will — anything can happen and it's O.K. Fantasies, like dreams, don't represent the real world, or necessarily what you want to have happen in the real world. Accept yourself in this most personal way.

And if you should get caught by someone who is uptight about it, don't defend yourself or make excuses — simply ask, "Tell me what you mean. Do you think it's wrong? I want to try to understand what you mean." Then let them talk, and when they are finished, ask again, "I'm not sure I know what you mean, tell me again, I'm trying to understand."

I think you will find a whole new sense of self-worth in the process, which is very much worth celebrating.

*   *   *   *   *   *   *

SOMETIMES IT'S SMART TO BE DUMB
(Jeffrey Whitmore)

Here's a story about a dumb boy and a smart uncle. Whenever the smart uncle came to visit, he would put a dime and a nickel in his hand and tell the dumb boy to take his pick.

The dumb boy would then examine them carefully and then, invariably, say, "I'll take the big one."

Invariably, the smart uncle would laugh and give him the nickel.

One day one of the dumb boy's friends said, "No wonder your uncle calls you dumb. Don't you know that a dime is worth twice as much as a nickel?"

The dumb boy looked around to make sure that his smart uncle was out of hearing range and answered, "Sure, but if I took the dime, my smart uncle would stop giving me nickels."

Moral: Sometimes it's smart to be dumb. Sometimes it's smart to be crazy, or awkward, or to behave in ways that make you seem much worse off than you are.

* * * * * * *

THE END

Once, my son Lars, when he was four years old, said:
"Sometimes I'm so happy, I sing in my heart!"
And I cried and laughed and melted — hearing him.

To have meaning, to succeed, is to get into the now — and out of the linear, logical language traps that the world sets for us.

You can't "sing in your heart" for a week — but you can for a moment, for a "now."

I hope that "now" you have read this book — the moments will explode for you as you "do you own thing" in using what is here in your own very special way!

My poet friend Ric Masten once said —
"We all will do what we must do, simply to exist!"
And that's so true —
I don't exist in the past or the future — I only exist now!
How about you, my friend?

*   *   *   *   *   *

Addendum
DRUGS, GUNS, CARS, SKATEBOARDS, SEX

Taking risks is really part of the way all of us find out who we are. It's especially true of teenagers. It's always been true of young people and I hope it always will and can be true of them. Pushing at the edges of what life is all about in order to find out who they are and how they want to live life is perfectly normal.

But, here's the rub. Kids can't be expected to know how risky things are — they don't have the experience or knowledge. You can't be expected to have a sense of the future and provide for it because you are so very much caught up in the "now" of life — what's happening to you "now" — hassles, hang-ups, happinesses, horrors!

When I was a kid, just about the most dangerous, risky thing a young person could do was to get pregnant or be the cause of someone's pregnancy. I had several friends whose lives were ruined forever because of that.

What's different for young people today is that there are so many more things that, when done by kids very innocently, just taking the risks they "need" to take in order to become persons in their own right, can ruin their lives forever. Large numbers of young people are paraplegic, quadraplegic, never able to walk again, dead, because of a seemingly innocent sport — skateboarding. An amazing number of Southern California "surfers" and "beechers" have cataracts by age 30 because of ultra-violet radiation contamination from the sun.

One of the sayings of the gunlover's lobby is, "Guns don't kill people, people do." They portray the gun as an innocent conglomeration of metal, wood, gunpowder, pretty to look at, fascinating to shoot, etc. Yet the facts are irrefutable — the very presence of a gun is so often the cause of a death. If it had not been there, no one would have died. It's so much harder to kill someone by punching them out. A bullet through the head is so final and irreversible.

Sure, it's normal for you to be taking risks! That's why the catch phrase, "Just say No" so often has the opposite effect. I want to plead with you (I'm on your side) to take seriously who you are and what you want to do with your life. So often, when young people get involved with drugs, sex, wild driving (one of my dearest friends will never walk again because of "a fun ride we were taking on a mountain road.") skateboards, guns, etc. — they can go over the line without ever realizing it, to the point where their future is irrevocably destroyed by what they have chosen to do. One of the ironies of this kind of behavior is that so often they are allowing someone else to control their lives rather than themselves. In a very realistic way, to do something as rebellion against parents is giving those parents the power to destroy your life. To do something, because all your friends are doing it, is to give them the power to decide your future for you.

As I've said earlier in this book, so much of becoming an adult is in beginning to make your own choices. Whatever you are choosing as you take the normal personality shaping risks that every healthy young person takes, ask yourself, "Is this something I really want to do?" or, "am I continuing to allow someone else to be in control of my destiny?"

* * * * * *